Warm and joyful stories from childhood

The Funny Things Kids Say

Will Brighten Any Day

Grace Witwer Housholder

*With Watercolors
by Debbie Rittenhouse*

Volume III

This book
belongs to
_____

The Funny Things Kids Say Will Brighten Any Day (Volume 3)

Published by the Funny Kids Project
816 Mott St.
Kendallville, IN 46755 USA

Grace Witwer Housholder
816 Mott St.
Kendallville, IN 46755 USA

International Standard Book Number: 0-9663006-0-2

Library of Congress Catalog Card Number: 98-96081

10 9 8 7 6 5 4 3 2 1
Printed in the United States of America

The text is 16 point Times typeface for easier reading.

Foreword

If you want to see humor in its best form, watch and listen to kids. Listen as they hear words used in worship and around the home, and share what their little minds do with adult concepts and theologies. I think that when the Lord suggested that we adults become like children, He was also suggesting that we recapture some of that childlike innocence and trust and fresh humor.

I have nothing against old people. I am getting to be one of them myself. But I am against grown-up people who have become "groan-ups," people who have lost the joy and celebration of life in the Lord.

I am convinced that God created laughter just to hear and see His creation enjoy life. Sure, laughter is healthy for you; it reduces stress; it helps you relax. But I think it is okay to enjoy laughing just because it is fun to do, with no other purpose.

This book is sure to bring many smiles and a few belly laughs. I hope that reading it encourages you to listen even more carefully to the children in your life and to savor and save the humorous things they say. Please fill the last pages with your own funny stories to create a keepsake volume that will be cherished for generations to come.

As you enjoy the humor of childhood, remember that children and laughter are gifts from God!

Dr. Richard Bimler
President of Wheat Ridge Ministries, author of *"Angels Can Fly Because They Take Themselves Lightly"*

Introduction

Laughter is a tonic! It helps reduce stress, increase creativity and build stronger relationships, especially in families.

The stories in this book are from the "Funny Kids" newspaper column I started in 1987. I am deeply grateful to the hundreds of families in northeastern Indiana and across the nation and Canada that have shared their stories with me.

If you have stories to share, I urge you to send them to me at 816 Mott St., Kendallville, IN 46755 USA.

The goal of the Funny Kids Project is to bring you smiles and laughter and to encourage you to listen more carefully to the children in your life. Please fill the last pages of this book with your own stories to create a keepsake volume that will grow in sentimental value over the years.

Shortly after my first "Funny Kids" book was published in 1994 I found a "Funny Kids" journal my great-grandmother, Grace Osburn, had kept. It has about 70 stories covering a 10-year span before World War II. For example, one time when my dad was 4 or 5, he put too much water in the radiator. His mom said if he had listened to her, it would not have run over. "I know you are more intelligent and older and more clever and have more experience," my dad told his mom. "But I know a good many things that you have forgotten!"

I hope this book brings back "things that you have forgotten" and helps you stay a kid at heart!

Grace Witwer Housholder

Table of Contents

For Dad, who told me
to write a column!

Thank You

I would like to express my deep gratitude to the hundreds of people who have shared their stories with me and to the wonderful people at Kendallville Publishing Company who have helped me with this book!

Chapter One

Kids and Their Creator

Children bring smiles when they talk about religion because of their simple faith and the way they translate everything they know into their own terms. For example, one child announced that he wants to take his swing set to heaven. We smile — but how do we know there aren't swing sets there? Children's simple, steadfast faith can be inspirational. Jesus said, "Let the children come to me, for the kingdom of God belongs to such as they." (Mark 10:14)

The vacation Bible school teachers were talking with some mothers who commented that the children really seemed to be getting that year's message. The song of the day was "Peace Like a River." On the way home Hannah, 2, started singing lustily in the car, "I got to PEE like a river..."

A little girl from an unchurched family was visiting a Sunday school class. She saw a picture of Adam and Eve.
"Who is that?" the little girl asked.
The teacher tried to explain the story of Adam and Eve.
"Humpf," the child said. "Looks like Tarzan to me!"

Adam, 6, always wore a tie to church. One Sunday someone commented how nice it was to see Adam so dressed up every Sunday.
"We never force him to put on a tie. He just does it," his grandma said.
"Well, yeah, Grandma," Adam piped up. "The last thing Grandpa always says before we leave every Sunday is 'Don't forget your ties and offerings!'"

Chapter One

Kenneth was trying to explain to Scottie about how God created the Earth.

"Well," Scottie asked as Kenneth concluded, "where did God stand when He was making the Earth?"

Rachel was telling her mother some of the Bible stories she had heard in Sunday school. After telling about Noah's ark, she added, "That was back in the '50s!"

When the Jellisons took their young children outside to see Comet Hale-Bopp, they were amazed at how quickly the children could find it.

Little Jalyssa commented, "It looks like God is shining His flashlight on us!"

Nathan, 3, told his grandma about the death of his family's cat, Rockie. He said: "Mommy took Rockie to the doctor, and the doctor gave him some medicine to make him sleep. And now he is in heaven, dead. But Rockie looks so cute with his little angel wings!"

After the funeral for his grandfather, Craig, 6, asked, "Do you know where fish go when they die?"

"Where?" his mother asked.

"They go to fish heaven," Craig said. "I know what Grandpa is doing right now... he's fishing for dead fish!"

Funny Kids

Jonathan, 5, and Jack, 3, were supposed to be getting ready for bed, but they couldn't seem to settle down. Their father sternly sent them to their room.

The weary parents overheard Jonathan say to Jack, "Now, fold your hands this way. We HAVE to pray...Dear Jesus, will you please give Daddy back his sense of humor in the morning!"

Sue took her 4-year-old granddaughter, Olivia, home. When they drove into the driveway Sue noticed some coins on the ground and picked them up.

"Where did that come from, Grandma?" Olivia asked.

"Oh, pennies from heaven, Olivia," Sue said.

Sue went into the house. When she came back out she saw Olivia with her hands up in the air, saying, "Send some more down, Jesus!"

One Sunday morning in church just as the choir performed a big finish to the hymn, in the dead quiet the small voice of Marrisa, 3, rang out: "E-I-E-I-O!"

A third-grade teacher in a Lutheran school was talking with his class about how last names developed over time. He made the point that people in the Bible did not have last names.

"For example," Mr. Buuck said, "take Abraham. What was his last name?"

One boy's hand shot up as he replied with excitement, "Abraham Lincoln!"

Chapter One

Bonnie was teaching a class of first-graders in vacation Bible school. As she shared the story of Abraham's travels with his nephew, Lot, one little boy leaned forward and blurted out: "But when do we get to the part about Abraham getting shot in that movie place?"

Norma, who has very bad arthritis, told relatives at a family gathering that when she gets to heaven she's going to ask God for a new pair of legs.

But Jael, 4, told Norma she won't need new legs in heaven, because she'll have a pair of wings!

Natalie, 2, asked whether the Easter Bunny "will be getting up with Jesus on Easter morning."

At church there was a guest speaker who talked about the importance of remaining a virgin until you are married. On the way home the 9-year-old girl said, "Mom is the only one I know who is a virgin!"

Kids' comments about heaven:
• A 5-year-old said, "Well, I know one thing for sure. When I go to heaven I'm going to take my swing set with me!"
• "When I get to heaven I'm going to ask God why he made mosquitoes," Kelsey said.
• "I can't wait to get to heaven, because then everything in Wal-Mart will be free," Rickey said.

Jeff, 5, told his parents that someone had said something bad. They asked what the person had said.

Jeff replied, "He said, 'Oh...'" Jeff paused and pointed upward. "'Oh... Him!'"

Patrick, 7, asked his mom if there are angels.

She said yes.

"Are they with me all the time?" he asked.

She said yes.

"Well, I tried to give one a cookie," Patrick said, "and it fell on the floor."

All the children were picking on each other. One of them was pulling the 3-year-old's hair.

The 5-year-old said, "Adam, quit pulling out her hair. Now God will have to start counting all over again!"

Caleb, 4, was eager to go to a large family reunion so he could play with all his cousins and enjoy all the good food everyone would bring. But his parents had vehicle problems, and at the last minute they had to stay home. So instead of a potluck with all sorts of wonderful food, Caleb had to stay home and eat leftovers.

As they sat down to eat, Caleb's mom asked him to say the blessing.

Caleb folded his hands, looked down at the food and then up at the ceiling. "God," he said, "I've got nothing to say!"

Chapter One

At the midweek service, the minister asked, "Is there anyone who is just bursting to give a testimony?"

Nancy, 4, quickly raised her hand.

"You?" her mother asked, wondering what spiritual truth Nancy would relate.

"Yes!" Nancy said urgently. "If you don't take me to the restoom I'm going to burst!"

One Sunday the pastor had a "testimony session." When the volunteer testimonials died down, there was an awkward silence. The pastor asked whether anyone else had something to say.

A little girl stood up and announced, "My mom is pregnant!"

A grandmother was babysitting her grandchildren during a severe thunderstorm. There was lots of lightning, and the children were scared.

"God will take care of us," the grandmother kept telling the children, but they were still upset.

When the children's parents returned, one of the children said, "Grandma, we don't need God any more. Dad's home!"

The Easter Bunny gave Carrie, 2, some plastic Winnie-the-Pooh characters. Carrie was examining them closely. "Mommy, Piglet is so skinny," she said. "I guess that's just the way God made him!"

Chuck, 6, was surprised to learn that Jesus didn't speak English. But then he figured it out. "That's right," he said, "America wasn't discovered yet!"

The Ley family was talking about guardian angels. "Who is my guardian angel?" Elizabeth asked her mother.

"Oh, it must be your great-grandfather," Linda said.

"Great!" Elizabeth said. "I WOULD have a dead one!"

Shawn, 3, was warned not to touch his aunt's cactus plants because they would prick his fingers.

"Who made the cactus?" Shawn asked.

"God did," his aunt replied.

"Didn't that hurt His hands?" Shawn asked.

During the children's sermon, a pastor was using a yardstick to illustrate the term "Golden Rule." The pastor mentioned that yardsticks have many uses, including spanking.

A daughter whispered to her father, "It wouldn't work on me! I have buns of steel!"

Carrie, 3, was pretending to read her Sunday school lesson, which was about Abraham. Carrie prattled on and then concluded, "And Abraham told Mary, 'Jesus will be back after these messages!'"

As he was driving past the cemetery with his mother, Matthew, 4, commented that there weren't many girls buried in the cemetery.

"What makes you say that?" asked his mother.

"Because there aren't many flowers on the graves," he replied. (He thought that only girls get flowers on their graves!)

Rebecca, 6, said the Lord's Prayer this way: "...Hollow be your name... MY will be done... forgive the trespasser, for MINE is the kingdom and the power and the glory..."

Rebecca's mom said it was no wonder Rebecca has trouble seeing herself as a sinner.

Jack, 4, was asked to say the table grace before the meal at a family gathering. He made the sign of the cross, folded his hands and began, "Now I lay me down to sleep."

Then he stopped and said, "Oh, my God, that's the wrong prayer!"

So he made the sign of the cross again and said, "Bless us, O Lord, for these thy gifts, which are are about to receive from thy bounty. Amen."

Jane taught Carrie, 3, the verse: "Do your best. God will do the rest."

One time after repeating the verse Carrie told Jane, "I want Jesus to do ALL of the work!"

Phyllis told her son Zak, 8, that he belonged to her.

"I'm not yours," Zak said. "God is letting you borrow me from Him!"

During a windstorm, the Scheibers' windows were making loud rattling and shaking noises.

The next morning Jane asked Carrie, 3, whether she had slept well. "Well, Mommy," Carrie said, "the wind really bothered me last night. But I prayed to Jesus that I wouldn't fly out the window without my coat on!"

During the children's sermon the pastor showed the children a phone book and asked them, "Can you contact God this way?" The kids said no.

All of a sudden one little girl said with great excitement, "Well, why don't you look under G?"

When Bob's son drew a picture of the crucifixion scene, Bob noticed that the picture had an airplane in the top corner.

"Son, this is a wonderful picture," Bob said. "But what is the airplane doing?"

"Dad, don't you know?" the boy replied. "That's Pontius Pilot!"

Bev was telling her 4-year-old son about the Easter season. When she started telling about Jesus, he said, "You mean they're after Him again?"

Ellen lived across the street from a church. There were dandelions on her lawn and on the pastor's lawn. Ellen jokingly told the pastor, "Well, you're just going to have to keep your dandelions on your side of the road, and I'm going to try to keep my dandelions on my side." A little girl in the church nursery overheard the conversation and said, "Don't you know what those dandelions are for? God put them out there to button down the grass!"

Faith, 3, went to Good Friday services. That night she prayed: "Thank you, Jesus, for dying on the cross. And thank you we didn't have to watch!"

Chapter One

The family was enjoying mushrooms at a special breakfast Carol had prepared.

"Isn't it wonderful that we found mushrooms in the woods!" Carol said. "It's like a free breakfast from God!"

Karl, 9, looked at Carol with a puzzled expression.

"They're not really free," he said. "Grandpa had to buy that woods, and it cost a lot of money!"

Barbara was driving with Casey, 4.

"Grandma, isn't the sky just beautiful?" Casey commented.

"Yes, it is," Barbara said. Then she decided to test Casey about his Sunday school lessons. "Who made the sky?" Barbara asked.

"Well, God did."

"If God made the sky, who made the oceans?" Barbara continued.

"Well, God did."

"If God made the oceans, who made you?"

"Grandma, don't you know?" Casey said. "God made me, and He made you... And God made paper towels, too!"

As the Farmer family was sitting around the supper table, Jennifer, 5, who was in kindergarten at Faith Christian Academy, turned to Andy, 3, and then pointed to their dad.

"That's not your real father," she said, startling the whole family.

"Yes, he is!" Andy said.

"No, he's not," Jennifer insisted. "God is your heavenly father."

Then pointing at their dad again, she said, "That's your homely father!"

Chapter Two

Kids' Word Mix-ups

One day as Michelle was preparing to take her two children to day care, she got a call just as she was walking out the door. She ended the call quickly by promising to call back later.

That afternoon, when she picked up the children, Jared, 5, was unusually quiet during the drive home. Suddenly he asked, "Mom, when are you going to get rid of Haley and me?"

Michelle nearly wrecked the car. Where could he have gotten such a horrible idea?

She asked Jared what had made him ask that.

He replied that that morning she had told the person who called, "Let me get rid of my kids, and I'll call you right back."

We adults need to think twice about everything we say within earshot of our children. As the word mix-ups in this chapter show, they can interpret things in some very unusual and unexpected ways. The results range from shocking to side-splitting!

Tara, 3, asked her mother, Gwen, what she was going to be for Halloween.

"I don't think I'm going to dress up for Halloween this year," Gwen said.

"What!" Tara exclaimed, "you're going to go naked!"

Jalyn and Jalyssa are twins. Jalyn was sick and missed a day of school. The next day the principal saw Jalyn, who she thought was Jalyssa.

"How is your sister feeling?" the principal asked.

"I am my sister," Jalyn responded.

Emily, 4, was brushing her teeth.

Her older cousin asked her whether she had lost any teeth yet.

"No," Emily replied. "I take good care of my teeth."

Leah (pronounced lee-ah) and her younger sister Lexie, 4, were visiting their grandparents.

"Those are nice leotards you have on," Lexie's grandpa said while he was holding her on his lap.

"Those aren't 'LEAH'tards," Lexie said. "They're 'LEXIE'tards!"

A grandmother was helping her granddaughter with a homework assignment about American wars. The grandmother said that the Redcoats of the Revolutionary War were called that because they wore red coats.

The granddaughter thought a minute and asked, "What color did the petticoats wear?"

Bashu, 5, went to a science workshop. Afterward he asked his mother, "Is it the law of gravity that keeps people from falling off the Earth?"

She answered yes.

"Well, what did people do before they passed the law?" he asked.

Ryan called Madelyn to announce that he had lost his first baby tooth. "How did you lose it?" Madelyn asked.

"I didn't lose it, Nanny," Ryan replied. "It's under my pillow!"

At the dinner table Don began to let off some steam that had built up from the day's office politics.

His 9-year-old son was surprised by his father's frustration. "But, Dad," he protested, "aren't you pretty high up in your company's anarchy?"

In Adventures in Learning, Caleb, 6, learned about a small fish that has the job of eating the debris off large fish.

"I need one of those for my belly button!" Caleb said.

"Bad Sterling!" Teresa told her little boy when he was misbehaving.

He turned around, looked at Teresa and said, "Bad boy, Mommy!"

"Watch the birdie!" someone said when the Balzer family was taking a family picture.

The photo shows Ron, 2, leaning back and looking up.

"What were you doing, Ron?" someone asked.

"I was looking for the birdie!" he replied.

Seija told Ian, 4, to turn down the television because his father was sleeping. She didn't realize that she was speaking rather loudly.

"Mom, turn down your lips. Dad's sleeping!" Ian said.

Chapter Two

Katherine was trying to squeeze some gloves onto 2-year-old Abbie's fingers. "Oh, Grandma," Abbie said, coughing. "These gloves are choking my fingers!"

When Nicole and Katie were toddlers their mother often bathed them together. She would use the suds to coil their hair up into a "bun," and tell the girls what she was doing.

One day Katie swept up her own hair and announced, "Look, Mommy! I have a piece of bread in my hair!"

Michelle overheard her two daughters as they were playing dress-up. One announced, "I'm the damsel under stress!" (Damsel in distress!)

Nathaniel, 4, was running around the back yard with his new gun, shouting, "Name, rank and favorite cereal!" (Name, rank and serial number!)

Alyssa, 3, was helping her dad put in a ditch beside the barn for water lines. The next day Alyssa's mother mentioned that Alyssa had gotten her shoes dirty while helping her father dig a ditch.

"Daddy said it was a road," Alyssa said.

"It was a ditch," her mother corrected her.

"No," Alyssa said, "Daddy kept saying, 'Get out of the road. Get out of the road!'"

Marty took her son, Mike, to vote with her. The voting was in a school that had lots of paper turkeys decorating the walls, because Thanksgiving was only a few weeks away.

While they were standing in line, Mike asked Marty what she was doing.

"I have to vote," she said.

"Which turkey are you voting for?" Mike asked.

In the 1940s, when Fritz was 2, he was riding in a car. He kept saying, "Fork, fork, fork, fork..."

His father couldn't imagine what Fritz meant until he got down to a child's-eye level in the car. Then he realized that all Fritz could see was telephone poles going by!

Cale asked his preschool teacher whether Catwoman is a girl or a boy.

Marcia, 3, was told her shoes were on the wrong feet. "These are the only feet I have!" she replied.

Graham wouldn't admit he was crying. "My eyes are just a little squirty," he said.

Ron was cleaning the car. He asked Andy, 5, to get him a damp rag. Andy ignored his father's words, so Ron had to ask for a damp rag several times.

Finally Andy went after it. "Okay," Andy said, "here's your damn rag!"

Chapter Two

Barry, 3, told his parents about the beautiful girl next door who had "dipstick" and "beefume!"

Kristi's babysitter told her that her mother was tied up at work, but would be coming soon.

"But they don't have rope where my mom works," Kristi said very seriously.

A little girl knew that when you aren't dressed you are in your "birthday suit." When she was changing into her swimsuit and saw a lady with no clothes on, she told her that she was in her "party suit!"

Penny had just brought home their newly adopted 6-year-old son from Thailand. Penny explained to Charlotte, 4, the girl next door, that Alex was from a country where they don't speak our language. And she asked Charlotte to help Alex learn English.

Charlotte marched over to Alex, got up close so he could hear her clearly, and said, "Okay, Alex, say English!"

Evy, a second-grader, was asked what she knew about Abe Lincoln. "I don't remember much," she said. Then she brightened. "But I do remember he had four fathers!" ("Four score and seven years ago our forefathers...")

A kindergartener told his teacher his new sweater had his name embroidered on. "It has a mammogram," he said.

Breeana wasn't feeling well. Her mother made her as comfortable as possible and left the room. Later, Breeana's little brother Ryan went in to check on Breeana and found her crying.

"Mom," he called. "You better come back in here! She is just crying her little hearts out!"

Ian, 4, made a Halloween costume that looked like an X-ray machine.

He proudly told his teacher, "I'm an excavator!"

Jeff, 5, saw the high school's version of "Cinderella." When it was over he asked, "Why did Cinderella always want to go to the mall?" Later he said his favorite character was the fairy godmother, because she had "bombs" — the fireworks that went off around her.

When Rebecca, 5, was playing pretend, she would say, "No Mom, this isn't for real; this is for fake!"

Jarrod, 8, saw a picture of the first footprints on the moon. And he spotted one special word: Neil.

"Dad, look!" he called. "Here's a picture of Shaquille O'Neal's footprints on the moon!"

A second-grader told her teacher she was certain whom her dad would vote for: Bill Lincoln!

Jeff, 5, asked his mom if she would sing his favorite song to him. "You know," Jeff said, "'Swing low, sweet Cheerio!'"

Elizabeth, 5, was very proud of what she was learning in preschool. "Grammy," she said, "now I can speak French and Spanish."

Sharon was surprised to hear this. "Say something for me in French," Sharon said.

"Shalom!" Elizabeth replied.

Katherine was driving with Abby, 3. "Gramma," Abby asked, "can we go down past the cemetery and see Paw-paw's flowers on his gravy?"

Mary enjoys teaching new things to her granddaughter Justine, 3.

Justine was going to be moving to Michigan, so Mary decided to give a geography lesson. She showed her a map of the U.S. and pointed out Indiana and Michigan.

"See, Michigan looks like a mitten," Mary said. "And see how Indiana looks like a sock."

Later Justine was all excited about showing her mother what she had learned. Her mother pointed to Indiana and asked, "Okay, what's this?"

With great pride Justine said, "A sock!"

Tish heard a commotion in the kitchen and ran to see what Seth was up to. He told her he was just messing around.

"Well, at least you are honest," Tish said.

Seth put his hands on his hips and said, "I am NOT Pocahontas!"

A little girl told her grandparents that the county's new sheriff was named Pat. They were puzzled, because they knew their newly elected sheriff was not named Pat. Later when the sheriff's car passed them on the highway the little girl got very excited. "See, there is our new sheriff, and his name is right there!"

Sure enough, the car said, "Sheriff 'Pat'rol!"

On a camping trip in Canada Scott told David, 3, "Let's kill two birds with one stone and go to the campstore for some well water and to buy you a treat."

When they left the store, David told the clerk, "Now we're going to kill some birds!"

As Zachary, 3, and his grandmother were driving through the parking lot, they had to maneuver over several speed bumps. After driving over the third one, Zachary said, "Mimi, your car has the hiccups!"

Thanks to her father, Tracye inherited several moles on and around her neck.

One night while sitting at the dinner table, LaTanya, 5, asked, "Mom, what are those things on your neck?"

"They are moles," Tracye politely replied. "I got them from my father's genes."

"Mom!" LaTanya scolded, "that's why you're not supposed to wear other people's clothing!"

Chapter Two

A little girl was shopping with her mother in a clothing store with a large display of mannequins. The little girl asked if they were real people. The mother said no.

"Did they used to be real?" the little girl asked.

Judy was playing Candyland with her niece, Alissa, 4. After a while Judy noticed that Alissa was cheating by drawing extra cards.

"You're cheating," Judy said.

"No, I'm not," Alissa said.

"If you're going to cheat I'm not going to play any more," Judy said.

"I'm not cheating," Alissa replied. "I'm winning!"

David, 3, looked so much like his dad that everyone told him he was "a chip off the old block." One day he proudly told his Grampa Jim, "I'm a chip off the old pot!"

Kristy told Cassie, 2, "You're silly!"

Cassie swung around, stomped her foot and said, "No, I'm CASSIE!"

Little Ryan had the reputation of always using too much toilet tissue. One day he came running, "Nana! Nana! The toilet is trying to throw up!"

Chapter Three

Purple Roses and Green Hearts

This is a story about my second-grade son and a little girl in his class whom I'll call Clarissa. Clarissa has long silky hair that her mother arranges in perfect curls. She is one of those little girls whom you look at and the word "perfection" comes to mind.

My son's older sisters discovered a few years ago that Paul thought Clarissa was a most special girl. When he was in kindergarten they teased him about his infatuation for her.

"Have you kissed her?" one of his sisters asked.

"NO!" he said.

"Have you held her hand?" another sister asked.

"NO!" Paul said again. But after a pause he added, "But I touched her chair!"

I forgot about Clarissa until a few days before Valentine's Day, when Paul got very interested in making Valentines on our home computer. The first one he made was for Clarissa. After he printed it out and folded it, he spent a long time coloring it. The roses were purple, the hearts were green, and he added an orange line drawing of himself lifting weights. When he was done, he wasn't satisfied, so he made another card and colored it more conventionally. I saved the first one.

That night he rummaged through a pile of things from my grandmother's house and found an old bottle of French perfume in a faded brocade box. The set was probably 30 years old. But perfume is not like wine — it does not improve with age. The perfume smelled like bug spray.

"Do you want this?" he asked me. I told him no. Then he went to each of his three sisters and asked them if they wanted the

29

old bottle of perfume. They all wrinkled their noses and said no.

When I found the perfume in his backpack, I put two and two together. "Is that for Clarissa?" I asked. He said yes.

The next day I asked him if he had given Clarissa the perfume. He said yes.

"What did you say when you gave it to her?" I asked.

"I said, 'Clarissa, nobody else wants this perfume. Do you want it?'"

Ah, the honesty of youth!

And the cruelty. A few days after Valentine's Day, Paul came home from school, ran upstairs to his bedroom, slammed the door shut and burst into loud sobs. It took a long time, but I finally got him to stop saying, "Go away," and learned that some of the boys in his class had teased him about Clarissa.

I'm not like those television moms who always know the right thing to say when a child is hurt, sad or confused. As I rubbed his back, I thought and thought about how to comfort him. I finally came up with, "It doesn't matter what other people think..." And then I remembered an article about how to teach children to react to bullies, and added, "If they tease you again, just look them in the eye and say, 'I don't like what you're saying. Please leave me alone.'"

After a while he stopped crying.

I pretty much forgot about Clarissa until yesterday, when Paul came to me with two tarnished, tangled necklaces he had gotten from the pile of stuff from my grandmother's house. "Does anyone want these?" he asked.

"Are they for Clarissa?" I asked.

"One's for Clarissa and one's for Madeline," he said.

"Why do you want to give a necklace to Madeline?" I asked.

"When I gave the perfume to Clarissa, Madeline said she wanted some, and now she wants a necklace."

I gave him permission to give the necklaces to Clarissa and Madeline. And I hoped the boys wouldn't find out about it.

Chapter Four

Kids and the Birds and the Bees

WillowDean took her grandson Scott, 4, to a restaurant. They were comfortably seated in a booth for two when Scott asked in a loud, clear voice, "Grandma, why is it that when my daddy and mommy go to bed at night they have jammies on. But when they get up in the morning they don't have them on?"

It seemed like the whole restaurant quieted down to hear WillowDean's response. She said, as calmly as she could, that sometimes the temperature changes at night and parents have to make adjustments.

Yes, sometimes we have to make adjustments in what we tell our children about the birds and the bees. But no matter how careful we are, it seems they are always one step ahead of us!

Amanda, 4: Daddy got you pregnant, didn't he?

Wanda: Yes!

Amanda: How did he do it?

Wanda: You'll learn about that when you get older.

Amanda: Was it magic?

Wanda: It was kinda like magic.

Amanda: So he just said, "I want Mommy to be pregnant" and you got pregnant.

Wanda (laughing): Something like that.

Amanda (worried): Uh-oh, Mommy. You might have two babies, because I said the same thing!

When Jacob told his third-grade class that his mother was expecting, Amanda asked him what he wanted the baby to be.

"A boy," Jacob said.

"What does your sister want?" Amanda asked.

"A girl," Jacob said.

"What does your mom want the baby to be?" Amanda asked.

"The last one," Jacob replied.

A boy proudly showed his teacher a photograph. "Here's a picture of our tomcat," he said. "She just had some kittens!"

Two weeks after her brother was born, Isabella, 3, asked Lucy, "Why do babies have the little droopy thing?"

"Droopy thing?" Lucy repeated. Then she realized what Isabella was talking about. "Not all babies have them," Lucy said. "Just boy babies."

"Just boys and men have droopy things?" Isabella asked. Then she continued knowingly: "Aleksander and Papa have droopy things. But you and I don't... We have ballerina bodies!"

Near the end of her pregnancy, Wendy had a long phone conversation with her mother, who lived several states away. Afterward she told Jacob, "Grandma asked me if I'm as big as a barn. Do you think I am?"

Jacob studied his mother. "No," he said. "A shed, maybe."

Ian, a second-grader, asked his mother what Labor Day is. "Is it when somebody really famous had a baby?" he asked.

Vi and Phil were talking when they mentioned the phrase "knowing the facts of life."

Chuck, 7, immediately jumped in. "I know the facts of life!" he said.

"You do?" Vi and Phil asked in surprise.

Chuck replied with a long list of the facts of his life: "You brush your teeth. You go to school. You eat healthy food..."

Patsy's 5-year-old son announced that he wants to be a bachelor when he grows up.

"What's a bachelor?" Patsy asked, surprised that her son had used that word.

"A bachelor is a man who goes around with a stick across his shoulder with a red hankie tied on the end with his clothes in it." (In other words, a hobo.)

Abby, 3, told her grandma that she had been thinking about whom she would marry.

"Well, marry someone rich," her grandma said.

Abby thought for a minute and then said, "I know, Grandma! I'm going to marry the Tooth Fairy!"

Carrie, 3, asked how God puts our bodies together. Before her mother could respond, Carrie said, "He doesn't have glue up in heaven!"

The Rasp family was playing a word game. Rebecca, 7, was asked to provide a word that begins with "H" that describes a very handsome man. Rebecca brightened, "H...O...T!"

Evan, 3, overheard a conversation between his parents about the possibility that their female dog, Kari, who was in heat, had gotten out and gotten bred.

"Mom, did Kari get bred from a male dog?" Evan asked.

"No," Ann said. "We don't think she did."

Evan continued, "Well, why would she want his bread?"

Little Ryan, who had just watched some karate on television, told the family that one guy kicked the other guy "right in the grins!" (He meant groin.)

Wendy, 3, was watching television with her father, Olen, when a commercial came on that showed a mother breast-feeding her baby.

"You used to eat that way," Olen said.

"I did not!" Wendy said indignantly. "I always use a fork!"

Cody, 4, was looking at an encyclopedia with his mother, Jennie. When they came across a picture of a baby in the womb, Jennie started talking about the umbilical cord and how the baby grows inside the mommy.

All of a sudden Cody sat straight up, pointed at the picture and said, "Hey! That baby doesn't have a diaper on!"

Chapter Five

A Class Act

From preschool to college, my children have been blessed with outstanding teachers. People who have not visited or worked in the classroom have no idea of the dedication and stamina teaching requires.

Getting an education is a hard job — but there are plenty of humorous moments, as these stories show!

It was a hot day at the beginning of the school year, and the first-graders had just trooped in from afternoon recess. They were lining up against the wall in the hall, taking turns at the drinking fountain.

A first-grade teacher overheard one of her students say to a friend: "What I want to know is, who signed me up for all day?!"

Jason's grandmother was driving him to first grade. As they approached the school, she noticed the flag was at half staff.

"I wonder why the flag is like that," she said.

"Maybe it's because we have half a day of school," Jason quickly replied.

On a fall day Quintin saw some geese and pointed out that they weren't quite flying in the proper V formation.

Rebecca, who had been working with her letter people in kindergarten, said matter-of-factly, "Maybe they haven't had that letter person in school yet!"

Daniel, 8, was writing a book report about "The Funny Things Kids Say (Vol. 2)."

"Did you really read it?" Ruth asked.

"I shouldn't have to," Daniel said, "because I starred in it." (He had one line in the book!)

During a class Valentine's party, a little boy said, "Where's Bob? Why isn't he here?"

Phyllis finally figured out that the boy meant the former principal.

The little boy shook his head and told Phyllis, "I just can't believe he's missing the best day of his life!"

"Let's begin reading," Phyllis said to the second-grader she was helping. "Will you turn to the story?"

"What channel?" the boy asked.

Jeff, 5, did something bad at school, and his teacher gave him a note to take home to his mother, Vi.

As Jeff handed Vi the note, he asked, "Is loving your mother more important than getting a note home from your teacher?"

Dana went in to wake up Samantha, 6, for school. In her sweet morning voice Samantha said, "Mom, you're so lucky you don't have to get up!"

When there was a school delay because of ice, Seija, who was at work, received a call from her daughter, Ashley, 8, who was being cared for by Kathrin.

"Can I have a friend over?" Ashley asked.

"Why are you still at home?" Seija asked with surprise.

"There's a school delay," Ashley said.

"I know there's a delay," Seija said. "But why are you still home?"

"There's a delay all day!" Ashley said.

"They goofed!" Kari, a kindergartener, said when she saw her school pictures. "They made a mistake! I know I smiled. I smiled really good, and they goofed!"

She was not smiling in her school picture.

Paul, 8, has no conception of the things his mother does all day. On the first day of school, his mother said, "'Bye, have a nice day!"

He said, "'Bye, Mom, have a nice nap!"

Chuck, 6, was asked what the best part of first grade was.

"Recess!" he exclaimed.

"And the worst part?"

"Missing recess!" his cousin Paul, 8, chimed in.

Laura, 6, told her grandparents that during Drug Awareness Week she had told her teacher that her grandpa didn't use drugs any more. He had stopped using drugs July 4. (That was the day he stopped smoking!)

Chapter Five

Breanna's essay about why she should be the editor of the school newspaper went this way: "I enjoy writting. I think that I would be a great editor because I get A's in writting and spelling."

A second-grade boy came up to Sally in the school cafeteria. "Mrs. Stolz," he said, "I dreamed about you last night."

"You did?" Sally said with surprise. "What was the dream about?"

"I can't tell you," he said.

"You can't?" Sally said. "Was I yelling at you?"

"No," he said in a whisper. "You didn't have any clothes on!"

Some fifth-grade girls created a class newspaper. This is what Rule No. 4 said: "Your final artical must be readible but not prof-read."

One of their sections was called "Good & Bad News." Most of the articles were rewrites from the town's newspaper. But sometimes they had trouble classifying their stories.

"Do you think this story is good news or bad news?" Kim asked. "The lady wrecked her car and went off the road. But she wasn't hurt."

A second grader was asked to read aloud the word k-n-e-w.

"Canoe," he said.

As the end of the school year approached, Paul, 7, a sports fanatic, overheard his sister in high school say she was really nervous about finals.

"Who you gonna play?" he asked her.

Carrie, 3, overheard her father, a school principal, talk about his difficulty in finding substitute teachers during a flu epidemic.

One day Carrie went to her mother, Jane, and said very seriously, "I need a substitute today, Mommy, because my cat is sick!"

Andrew, a third-grader, noticed that the kindergarten class had two teams for the reading program. Then all of a sudden he figured out that the teacher had morning and afternoon students. "That's right," he said, "she has an A.M. class and an F.M. class!"

Two 6-year-olds were delighted to be participating in the science fair – until they found out there are no rides at the science fair.

The preschool teacher gave Zakk a crayon without a wrapper around it. "Teacher!" he exclaimed, "You gave me a naked one!"

Phyllis asked a first-grade girl to tell her about a library book her mother was supposed to read to her.

"Oh, I don't know," she said. "I was asleep when my mom read it to me."

Two first-graders were playing a math game while several other students watched. One was losing. In frustration he accused the boys of telling his opponent the answers, which they denied.

"Well, maybe not," he conceded. Then he blurted out, "But I know you're praying for him!"

Chapter Five

The children read the words: "This is my home."

"I can read it backwards," Keith said. "This is not my home."

Mary had just finished explaining the homework assignment to her second-graders when she saw Eric's hand waving in the air.

"Please don't send home all that homework," he said. "My mom won't be able to do it!"

With great excitement Dana asked her parents if they knew that a pound of crushed cans weighs the same as a pound of cans that aren't crushed!

Some fifth-graders were working in small groups, discussing Lincoln. One of the questions was, "What was the most famous speech Lincoln gave?"

One of the students asked tentatively, "Now what was that title — 'Getting the Birds a Dress?'" (The Gettysburg Address)

After Diane was done teaching her fourth- and fifth-graders about Lewis and Clark, all the students but one left for recess. The girl approached Diane's desk and quietly said, "I didn't want to say anything in front of the whole class, but it's Lois and Clark!"

Chapter Six

Money Matters

It is a tremendous accomplishment for a parent to teach a child the value of a dollar and the importance of managing money well. Children have no natural comprehension involving dollars and sense. It's all non-cents!

When the Ruperts installed their new computer system, their 7-year-old was really excited. "We're rich!" he exclaimed. "Now we can print our own money!"

"I don't have the money right now. Money doesn't grow on trees," a mother told her daughter.

"Well, Nathan," the 6-year-old told her younger brother, "we're just going to have to talk to those trees!"

Brittany had seen someone flipping coins for heads or tails. She bounced a quarter in front of her babysitter and asked, "Heads or buildings?"

Tracy, 4, wanted her mother to buy her something.

"I can't afford it," Jan said.

"Write a check!" Tracy suggested brightly.

Jan said she didn't have enough money in her checking account. So Tracy said, "Go to the gas station... You can get money there. You always say, 'Give me $10!'"

Jan explained she was asking for $10 worth of gas, not $10!

Chapter Six

Upon losing his fifth tooth, Dustin told his mother that he wanted to write a letter to the Tooth Fairy saying, "Please don't leave any money. I don't need any more."

Paul, 7, heard about Dustin's letter. A few days later when he lost a tooth, he said he wanted to write a letter like Dustin did.

This is the letter Paul wrote:

"i need 20$"

Morris told his grandson Ryan, 5, that he could put his tooth under his pillow and the Tooth Fairy would replace it with a quarter.

"A quarter, Grandpa?" Ryan asked. "Josh and Jeremie got $3 each from the Tooth Fairy for theirs!"

Audrey, 6, noticed her grandpa's striped socks. He said he had another pair just like them.

"Oh, you must be rich!" Audrey exclaimed.

Little Brittney said she was thinking about having a phone installed in her room. Bee asked her how she would pay for it.

"I'm not sure," Brittney said. "Maybe I'll drive my Barbie car down to the bank and get some money out!"

While playing Monopoly with his sister, Paul, 7, noticed that her money supply was dwindling to practically nothing.

"Catherine's going bank-robbed (bankrupt)," he said.

Out of the blue, Ian, 7, asked his mom, "When you and Dad die, who gets all your stuff?"

Startled by the question, Ann decided to answer the question with a question.

"Why?" Ann asked. "Is there something you want?"

"Yes," Ian said. "I want Dad's pocket knife."

"Well, Evan, is there something you want?" Ann asked their younger son.

"Yes," Evan said quickly, "I'll take the money!"

When Heidi was 5 her mother decided to give her $1 a week if she kept her room clean. Week by week Heidi saw the amount of money in her money jar grow, but one week she didn't clean her room, and Cindy told her she wouldn't get her dollar.

Heidi took a long look at her jar, and then pulled $1 out. "That's okay, Mom," she said. "You clean my room, and I'll pay you a dollar!"

Scott, 3, knew that his dad, who was a surveyor, often drew pictures at work. He also knew that his dad obtained money by working. So when they were low on money, Scott had the solution: "Why doesn't Dad just draw more money?"

After Clark Ream of People's Federal Savings Bank spoke to a fourth-grade class about checking accounts and how to write checks, he asked the students if they had any questions.

Right away a girl asked, "Were you a banker during the Great Depression?"

Chapter Six

Dustin's parents took him to the Shedd Aquarium in Chicago for a Christmas present. Dustin loved all the exhibits. But when they got to the penguin area, he left his seat and went right up to the rail that separated the audience from the glass. It seemed like Dustin just couldn't get close enough to the penguins.

Then Dustin called Fred down to join him.

"Dad," Dustin said, pointing to just beyond the railing, "there's a dime down there, and I can't quite reach it!"

While spending several days with us, my nephew Jeff, 7, who lives on a farm, lost a tooth. I asked him what the Tooth Fairy usually brings. "Well, twice she forgot," he said. "But usually it's a coloring book or a wooden yo-yo."

The next morning when he woke up and found a dollar under his pillow, Jeff told me that there is a City Tooth Fairy and a Country Tooth Fairy. "In the city you get money," he explained, "and in the country you get things!"

Scott, 6, wanted his mother to help him with something, but Cathie said she was busy with Sam, 2.

After Cathie repeatedly told Scott she was busy with Sam, Scott commanded: "Sell him!"

Jason noticed a Corvette his father had for sale on his used-car lot. "Dad," Jason said, "I'm seven now, you know, and it's time we started looking for a car for me."

"Really?" Lance said. "What did you have in mind?"

"How much is that Corvette on your lot?"

"Twelve thousand dollars."

After a moment of silence, Jason asked, "If I give you the $12 now, can I give you the thousand later?"

Chapter Seven

Kids and Weather

It's not nice to fool Mother Nature, we've heard in a popular television commercial. But Mother Nature fools us all the time. She especially fools kids, as these stories show!

During a typhoon in Guam, Adam, 8, told his brother, "Look, Kevin, the palm trees are doing a limbo dance with the telephone wires!"

When the 6-year-old daughter of missionaries from Africa saw snow for the first time, she exclaimed, "Oh, look! Ice cream everywhere!"

When David, 3, saw snow for the first time, he ran to his mother and announced with alarm: "Mom, the clouds fell down!"

On a beautiful sunny morning during Christmas break, Paul, 8, woke up and quickly looked out the window.

"Darn!" he said with a scowl on his face.

"What's wrong?" I asked.

"The sun is shining brightly," he said angrily.

"I like the sun," I said.

"I don't," Paul said. "It's going to melt the snow!"

Chapter Seven

As he entered a chilly lake in early summer, Brad, 3, screamed, "Mommy, get the teakettle!" (A teakettle of hot water is what his mother uses to warm up his wading pool at home.)

During a brief hailstorm, small white crescent-shaped pieces of ice bounced against the windows. Paul, 10, commented: "Someone's clipping their toenails!"

Jane was reading "Peter Rabbit" to Carrie, 3. Carrie noticed that Mother Rabbit was carring an umbrella under her paw.

"Why is she carrying an umbrella?" Carrie asked.

"Maybe she heard it's going to rain," Jane replied.

"Mommy," Carrie chided, "I don't think rabbits listen to the forecast!"

When the sun shone so brilliantly on the ocean that it looked like it was covered with diamonds, Paul, 10, said, "Mom, take off your sunglasses and look at the water. You know what I'm going to tell my kids — if I have any kids: that one day I saw little pieces of the sun fall into the water!"

During a bad storm, Phyllis told Nathan they would have to go to the basement until the storm was over. Nathan rushed to get his brother Ron from in front of the TV. He yelled, "Hurry, Ron, you and me and Grandma have to go down to the basement and keep the house from blowing away!"

One summer there were fires on Long Island, N.Y., and then reports of a hurricane in the Atlantic Ocean.

"What direction do hurricanes go in?" Bryan, 8, asked his mother.

"I don't know," Mary said.

"Well, I know where they should go," Bryan said. "They should go to New York and put the fires out!"

As he was walking to his babysitter's house on a sweltering summer day, Nathaniel, 3, said, "It's so hot my feelings hurt!"

One morning after his mother had turned on the window defroster on a chilly fall day, Jacob, 9, studied the heater buttons intently and asked, "Mom, which one is the toe defroster?"

Vi was helping Jeff get into his new snowpants. She told him they were waterproof.

"Are they bulletproof, too?" he asked.

Katherine, 5, heard the weatherman say, "Spring is just around the corner."

She went to the window and looked out for a while. "The weatherman lied," she said. "Spring isn't coming around OUR corner!"

On a warm spring day, Seth, 2, saw fluffy clouds scuttling across the blue sky. Reaching up, he told his mother that he wanted to get "some of the snow in the sky!"

Chapter Seven

Diane took her sons to the basement during a tornado warning. After 15 minutes of searching the basement, Mark, 3, said, "I don't see no tomato!"

While watching his uncle mix colors to paint a landscape, Tom asked, "Uncle Kenny, what color is thunder?"

Shawn's mother was putting him to bed one night when it was storming. "Do you know what thunder is?" Shawn asked.

Kerry said no.

"It's Jesus bowling," Shawn said. "And lightning is when Jesus gets a strike!"

Chapter Eight

Kids and Food

Some studies show that as few as one percent of the nation's children eat a truly balanced diet. Of course, what does "balance" mean? Balance is in the mind of the muncher. My son Paul thinks he eats a balanced meal when he has equal amounts of "soft" (brownies) and "hard" (pretzels). Or equal amounts of "salt" (potato chips) and "sweet" (cookies). But I never give up trying to get him to try different fruits and vegetables, in the hope that somehow, someday, he might acquire a taste for some of them.

One day Catherine, 10, was enjoying some fresh parsley, and I thought Paul, 7, might like to try some. "Paul, do you like parsley?" I called.

"Who's she?" Paul asked.

Cole, 4, went to a restaurant with his mother, Marci. She ordered him a grilled cheese sandwich and a soda pop.

When he heard what his mother had ordered for him, Cole started to cry.

"I don't want a girled cheese," Cole said. "I want a BOY cheese!"

Les was 3 when he was given his first ice cream cone. He very carefully ate all the ice cream and then licked the inside of the cone clean. Then he handed the cone back to his aunt and said, "Here's your vase back!"

Shawn, 4, told his mother he wasn't thirsty, "but I'm really hungry for something to drink."

Terry made some chicken noodle soup for himself and Paul, 8. When Terry took his first sip, some of the hot soup went down the wrong pipe, and he started to cough violently.

Paul looked at his choking chef/father and said, "You must have put germs in it!"

Emily always picked at her food. To help encourage her to eat, her mother, Laurie, frequently mentioned to her the poor, starving children in Africa. "Children are starving, and you are wasting this food," she often told her.

The last time Laurie ever told Emily about the starving children was the day Emily sweetly asked, "Aren't they dead yet, Mommy?"

While her mother was placing her order at a fast-food restaurant's drive-up window, Carrie, 3, asked, "Mommy, how do they get inside that box?"

Kara, 5, tried her great-grandmother's deviled eggs and decided that she liked them. "Grandma," Kara asked, "do you have any more of those doubled eggs?"

Katie was given some orange juice with pulp in it. When her father asked her why she didn't finish it, she said, "I don't like it with feathers in it!"

Nathan, 3, said, "I want some Yes Salt for my food. Grandpa gets the No Salt."

"Which dessert do you want?" Martha asked her granddaughter.

Abby pointed to a picture of a chocolate-butterscotch sundae. "Oh, you want a sundae," Martha said.

"No...I don't want to wait until Sunday!" Abby said.

Tyler, 7, was enjoying his meal in a seafood restaurant. But he didn't know about "those puppy things" (hushpuppies).

"Are they made out of real puppies?" he asked.

Upon receiving barbecue-flavored potato chips for the first time, a little girl complained that she had been given "rusty potato chips!"

Patrick had eaten something salty one evening, and he kept coming to his mother for some water or juice.

After repeatedly getting something to quench his thirst, Patrick said, "Mom, I think I have a drinking problem. I keep saying I need something to drink!"

The Klopfenstein family was sitting in a restaurant. After a while Trent asked very seriously, "Why are they called waiters when WE'RE the ones who have to wait?"

Kyle, 3, asked that the "raisins" be removed from his water-melon slice.

Speaking of raisins, when Carolyn made raisin-oatmeal cookies for her grandaughter, she said, "Oh, Grandma, there's BUGS in these cookies!"

A mother was amazed to learn that her daughter thought pickles came from trees.

"From trees?" the mother exclaimed

"I thought people picked pickles from trees," the daughter said. "You know, 'Peter Piper picked a peck of pickles...'"

Shea's great-grandmother was fixing spaghetti. The long sticks fell on the counter, and Shea picked one up and ate it. A little while later he came back into the kitchen and asked, "Do you have some more of those noodle sticks?"

To get Erica, 4, to take bites at supper, Michel says, "Can you take a bite for Mommy?" And Erica will usually comply.

One day Michel was in a hurry to get somewhere, and Erica wanted a snack. So Michel took one for her to eat in the car.

"Erica, that looks good," Michel said. "May I have a bite?"

"I just took one for you," Erica replied. "Did it taste good?"

Zane asked for some "bikini bread" (zucchini bread). While he was eating it, he said his piece had grass in it.

Cathie spent all afternoon baking cookies with Scott, 4. When they were done they had cookies all over the kitchen.

"Mom, we have a storm of cookies in here!" Scott said.

Lisa realized that maybe they were going overboard on their fast-food eating when their car broke down. She told Brea, 5, that they couldn't go anywhere that night.

"Well, how are we going to get supper?" Brea asked.

A first-grader said that he had only diet soda pop and vegetables for Thanksgiving. "I'm a veterinarian," he explained.

Rachel, 13, asked Zak, 7, why he was eating so much. "I'm chubbing up for winter," he said.

Jonathan decided to made Rice Krispies treats. As he read the list of ingredients to his mother, he called out, "I need 20 ozones of marshmallows!"

Catherine went to a drugstore that had a soda fountain — a new experience for her. When the druggist asked her what she wanted, she said, "Oh, give me a Pabst Blue Ribbon!"

Joel, 5, was asked to say the grace at Easter dinner. He prayed, "Thank you, Lord, for this good food, and thank you for sending Jesus to die on the cross for my sins, even though it was before my time. Amen."

Chapter Eight

While Julie was preparing supper, Kyle, 5, asked if he could help. Julie told him he could break the lettuce into little pieces and put the pieces in a bowl.

While Kyle was doing this, his father happened to ask him if he had washed his hands before handling the lettuce.

"No," Kyle replied, "that's okay. I always get my hands dirty doing this anyway!"

Lauren, 8, and Colton, 5, were sitting at the kitchen counter eating popsicles. Grandpa McCoy pointed out a piece of popsicle that had fallen under Colton's chair.

"I don't think it's mine," Colton said. "I think it's from Lauren."

"How could that be when it's under your chair?" Grandpa McCoy asked.

"Well," Colton said, "I think it fell diagonally!"

Chapter Nine

Winter Days Blurrr Together

This column was first published Jan. 24, 1983. It brings back warm memories of the days when my little ones were close to me and I could have a sticky hug simply by asking, "What is love?"

Sometimes I feel like I'm hibernating.

On certain sub-zero days when the three of us — 2-year-old, 4-year-old and 30-year-old — are snuggled in a Smurf quilt re-reading picture books, I feel like a mother bear with her cubs. Our days indoors take on a haziness and laziness that can only be compared to dozing. While others build up their blood pressure by pushing stalled cars or walking against gale-force winds, we leisurely look at a bug book or discuss the seasons.

After asserting it will be "very cold five more days" (she heard it on the Bozo weather report), the 4-year-old told me summer will come, "then Easter, then mosquito-time, then Halloween, then Christmas."

Our winter days follow a pattern that varies only slightly. In the mornings after Sesame Street and Bozo there are a couple of hours of playing house or school or vacation. Whatever the game, the 2-year-old hugs two dolls swaddled in her own diapers and the 4-year-old tells the three of them what to do.

Lacking a fireplace or a woodburning stove, most of the activity centers around the hot-air registers in the living and dining rooms. It is a major event when the heat kicks on. If the girls are not on the registers already, they quickly arrive and plop down with their dolls, wagons, books, blankets and hats.

Sometimes after the excitement of the first rush of hot air has worn off and the girls have departed for other pursuits, I realize we are paying $160 a month to melt the fire truck or roast the dolls they have left behind on the hot metal.

But I have found confinement is good for mother-daughter relationships. My efforts at conversation often bear unexpected fruit. In anticipation of Valentine's Day, I asked the 4-year-old, "What does love mean?"

"It means you give someone a flower," she replied.

I asked the 2-year-old the same question. She grinned and gave me a bear hug.

I guess I feel like I'm hibernating because in the spring, summer and fall we take daily walks to the park, library, uptown or just around the neighborhood. I love to walk — to chat with neighbors, watch the flowers and trees advance through the seasons, spot a turtle crossing the sidewalk, window-shop and perhaps stop for cookies on the way home. We return tired but refreshed.

In winter it takes a special surge of adrenaline — which I rarely have — to bundle the three of us from head to toe to plow through the snow for 15 minutes at best. We have no stamina in the cold.

Usually it is possible to drive places, and we venture out now and then. But the trips are short, and we make a beeline home. When there is ice or fresh snow on the road, I'm scared. I know all too well the sensation of not being able to turn or stop and sliding slowly into a snowbank. The girls sometimes sense my problems. Their reactions range from "This is fun!" to "Dear God, please help Mommy!"

In the afternoons we nap. I start out by reading, but frosted windows, the sound of a ticking clock and the soft rumble of the furnace are so conducive to sleep.

And so the days blur together, with little remarkable to distinguish them. Outside our window we see children walking to school, people driving to work, the postman making his rounds. But we three are hibernating — resting up for mosquito time.

Chapter Ten

Missed Manners

Kids say what they mean and they mean what they say. The little white lies that adults tell in order to be polite or to avoid hurting someone's feelings will never come from a kid's mouth. For example, if you're starting to get bald, a kid will be the first to tell you. When her parents had guests for Sunday dinner, Elizabeth, 5, took a sidelong look at Dr. Chandler and asked, "What happened to the other half of your hair?"

If you've got wrinkles, a child may tell you your skin "doesn't fit!"

Here are some bloopers that would definitely make Miss Manners turn pale.

Schlemmer's hardware store gives children free balloons. After Diane Schlemmer handed one little boy his free balloon, his dad prompted him by asking, "What do you say?"

The boy looked up at Diane and said, "Will you blow it up?"

When Jared was 3 he developed a love of the phrase "damn it," one of the unfortunate side effects of spending time with older cousins. Not wanting him to be a smart-mouthed kid who says, "That's a BAAAD word" to total strangers at ball games, Michelle told him it's a word only for grown-ups.

A little while later Michelle noticed that Jared was deep in thought. "Whatcha thinking about, buddy?" she asked.

"Oh," Jared replied. "I was just thinking that when I grow up I'm going to be a green frog, a green clown, a green elephant (green was the color of the week)...and I'm going to say 'damn it' all day long!"

Chapter Ten

A first-grader proudly told Mrs. Balzer, "I know how to burp now whenever I want to!"

The principal called Joey's mother because Joey had committed a serious offense.

"I'm afraid Joey was caught writing dirty language on the wall," the principal explained after Joey's mom arrived.

"No, I didn't," Joey protested. "The dirty word was already there. I just added the 'you.'"

Tanya was wearing a purple one-piece outfit. Her daughter, Abby, 18 months, walked around the kitchen counter so she could see all of her mother. After she tilted her head and carefully studied her mother, who was in purple from head to toe, Abby said, "Hi, Barney!"

In the middle of a wedding for one of our cousins, Paul, 8, turned to me and whispered loudly, "Whad'ya get 'em?"

As softly as I could I whispered to him, "A picture frame."

Paul loudly whispered back, "Shoulda given 'em Volume 2!"

John, 6, was visiting his neighbor Jim while he was doing yardwork.

"Jim, you look old," John said.

"How old do you think I am?" Jim asked.

"Fifty."

"I'm older than that."

"How old are you?"

"Sixty-five."

"Well, you're old enough to be dead!"

Colin, 4, continually hears the question, "Where did you get that red hair?"

His answer is always the same: "My Grandpa Dick." Grandpa's once-red hair is now gray, and there isn't much left of it.

At a family holiday party, the topic of red hair came up. Once again Colin heard the question: "Where did you get that red hair?"

Very seriously Colin looked at Grandpa Dick and said, "I will give you back some of your hair, Grandpa, since I took it from you, because you don't have much hair any more!"

Shawn, 4, was working himself through a crowd. When he reached his mother, she told him he should have said, "Excuse me."

"But I didn't burp," he said.

Audrey's mother told her to straighten up her room before her friend came over. "You don't want your little friend to see your room all messy, do you?" her mother asked.

"Well, I'll just shut the door," Audrey said.

Joseph, 4, got into trouble for swearing while he was reading a book to himself.

When his parents asked him why he had cussed, he said, "It fit the situation."

"I think I need a facelift to get rid of these wrinkles," Bunny told her daughter-in-law.

Jeanne, 8, overheard the conversation. "Yeah, Grandma," Jeanne said. "You could play tic-tac-toe on your face!"

Chapter Ten

A little boy was visiting his mother in the maternity wing of the hospital. He saw a very large-breasted nurse, stopped her and said, "I bet you can feed lots of babies with those things!"

A little boy said "Thank you" to an adult who had given him something.

"Don't mention it," the adult said.

The little boy said, "But my mama told me to."

The Gages invited Grandpa Gage for dinner before his trip to Mexico. Cassie, 5, was asked to say the blessing.

"Thank God for Mom and Dad," Cassie began. "And thank God for the food we are about to partake. And thank God Grampa is going to Mexico!"

Peggy likes to play a game called "piggy snort" with Rachel, 3. Her husband, Frank, who was raised in the South, is very big on manners, and he thinks the game (which involves snorting through your nose) is rude.

But he finally allowed Peggy to play "piggy snort" with Rachel if she would say "Sir!" or "Ma'am" after snorting.

So Peggy snorted at Rachel and said, "Sir!"

Rachel replied, "I'm not a SIR! I'm a MAMMAL!"

A mother let her son use the men's restroom by himself for the first time. Everything seemed fine until she heard a loud call that echoed through the restaurant: "Mom, come and wipe me off!"

Chapter Eleven

Bathroom Humor

Potty training is one of the most trying aspects of parent-hood. Some parents have the incredible good fortune to have kids who train themselves and also like to brush their teeth and comb their hair and take baths. But for most parents, tackling those things is a real struggle.

You can always tell which children are in the midst of potty training. At the Norfolk Zoo in Virginia, a number of families with small children gathered for a demonstration about elephant care. Young and old intently watched as the zookeeper explained how big elephants are, how they are washed, what they eat, etc.

Suddenly the elephant responded to nature's call, and several large piles came out its back end.

"I'm so proud of you!" a 2-year-old cried joyfully from the audience.

Paul, 8, detested taking baths. He always had an excuse, such as "I'm too tired," "I'm too busy," or "I already took a bath (yesterday)."

One night after coming in from playing, he came up with a new reason to avoid soap and water. "I don't need a bath," he said. "I'm going to get dirty again tomorrow!"

Breeana was hot and sweaty from playing outdoors. Her mother told her to take a bath.

Breeana was incensed. "Mom, I planned ahead," she argued. "I washed everything twice last night!"

Candice, 3, spent several hours playing with her dolls and stuffed animals. That evening when it was time for her bath, Candice refused to take one. Her mother said she had to.

"But I'm a doctor," Candice said. "Doctors only wash their hands!"

Taylor, 3, found his grandmother in the garage and asked her what she was doing.

"I'm working," Janice said. "Boy, Taylor, Grandma is pooped!"

All of a sudden Janice felt Taylor's little hand pat her backside. "Hold still," Taylor commanded. "I check to see if you pooped. You NO pooped!"

Then he ran off to play.

Carrie wet her training pants. Her exasperated parents asked her why she didn't tell them she needed to go to the bathroom.

She said, "I couldn't get the words out of my mouth!"

Before they left for a long drive, Carrie's parents asked her whether she needed to go to the bathroom.

"I don't have to go," Carrie, 3, said. "But I will write it down on my calendar so I can remember!"

Alexander, 3, came to his uncle with messy pants. Richard scolded him, but Alexander would not admit guilt.

With a straight face, Alexander told Richard that his younger sister, Ava, did it!

Bee gave Aimee, 4, a bath, but she didn't dry Aimee to her satisfaction.

"If you don't dry me better, I'll rust," Aimee told Bee.

"My body burped," a pre-schooler said when she expelled some gas.

As she changed her grandson's diaper, a grandmother said, "Now I just have to wipe off your little wee-wee."

He looked at her seriously and said, "Grandma, that's a BIG wee-wee!"

Emily, 2, had just soiled her diaper.

"Go to Mommy and get your diaper changed," Ben, 4, said.

"It is not," Emily said.

"Is too," Ben said.

"Is not."

Totally exasperated, Ben said, "Look at me! Why am I arguing with someone half my age?"

One day Brandy discovered the family's beautiful white Persian cat covered with beige make-up foundation. She found Alyssa, 3, and asked her what she had done to the cat.

"I give cat make-over," Alyssa proudly replied.

Tyler, 4, came to his grandmother. "I've got some good news and some bad news," he told her. "The good news is that I got your necklace out of the toilet, and it doesn't have anything on it!"

Chapter Eleven

To make apple butter, Ginger put apples, cinnamon and sugar in the crock pot to cook overnight. The next morning Patrick said, "Boy, Mom, the house smells like the Apple Festival. And I'm not talking about those horses' butts, either!"

Daniel, 6, attended an afternoon baby shower. That night, when it was time to take a bath, he tried to get out of it by saying that he had already had a "shower" that afternoon!

A grandmother was keeping her granddaughter for several days. One night the little girl tiptoed to her grandmother's bed and gently touched her. "Grandma, Grandma," she said softly, "I went to the bathroom, but I didn't flush because I didn't want to wake you."

Daniel's father, Mike, overheard Daniel, 3, and his nephew Colton, 4, carrying on a conversation while using the urinals in a public restroom.

"Mine is the Tasmanian Devil!" one boy said.

"Mine is Superman!" the other boy said.

Mike discovered that they were comparing the prints on their underwear.

Holly, 4, had a bedwetting problem, and she was used to seeing her mother strip her bed every morning. One morning Holly saw her mother changing the sheets in the master bedroom.

Holly put her hands on her hips and in her best "mommy" tone asked, "Who wet YOUR bed last night?"

The Gallery

The Miracle of Organ and Tissue Donation

Had it not been for the miracle of organ/tissue donation, Debbie Rittenhouse, the illustrator of this book, would be blind.

Debbie, the mother of four and a pastor's wife, has had corneal transplants in both eyes. "I'd love to be able to tell the families of the donors what wonderful gifts they gave," Debbie says. "Until you are on a waiting list, you don't take organ and tissue donation that seriously."

There are no guarantees that Debbie's corneal problems won't recur. "It's a little bit scary," Debbie says. "But I trust that God will take care of me. He has already worked miracles in both eyes."

Debbie knows that sight is a gift from God, and that as long as God wants her to paint, He will supply her with the gift of sight.

+++

If you have not yet done so, please talk about organ and tissue donation with your family. Physicians and hospital personnel can answer your questions and give you brochures about organ and tissue donation.

If you want to be an organ and/or tissue donor, it is important that family members know your wishes, because they are the ones who will be asked to make the decision.

Debbie Rittenhouse
Grace Witwer Housholder

A Message from a Donor's Father

A journalist, Becky, the third child of Mike and Fran DeWine, was killed in a car accident in 1993. She was an eye donor.

"People often face the crucial decision about organ donation at the worst possible time — after the sudden loss of a family member. Our family had never talked about the issue until we were left with no choice.' Families need to become aware of the life-saving difference they can make by deciding to become organ donors. Our greatest challenge is to ensure that more families understand how they can help save someone's life."

United States Senator Mike DeWine of Ohio

(Remember that signing an organ donation card is not enough. Consent of a family member or next of kin is required for a donation. Please make it a priority to talk with your family about organ and tissue donation. Share your life!)

The vacation Bible school song was "I've Got Peace Like A River." Mandy was singing, "I've got GEESE on a river!"

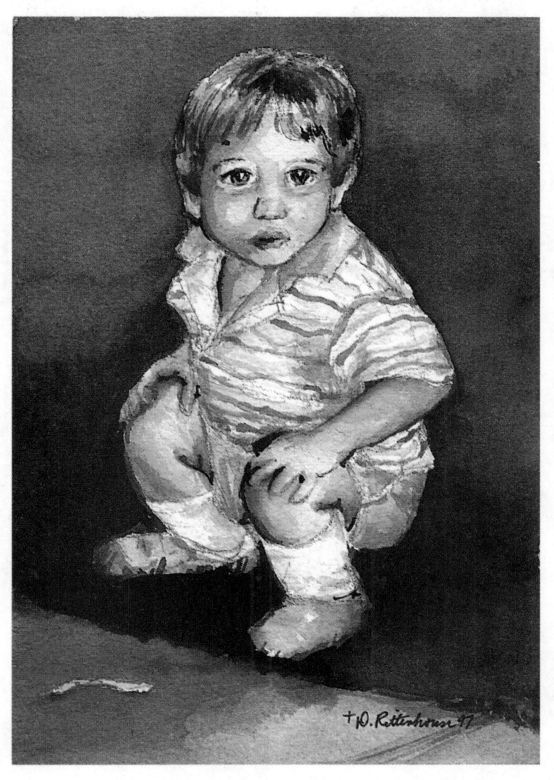

The dead worm was dried to a crisp. "That worm needs some exercise!"

"I just cleaned my sunglasses with tongue water and the bottom of my T-shirt!"

"I'm the damsel under stress." (Damsel in distress!)

"Yes, I got a hit...But he hit me first!"

"Well, I know one thing for sure. When I go to heaven I'm going to take my swing set with me!"

"You know what I'm going to tell my kids — if I have any kids — that one day I saw little pieces of the sun fall into the water!"

"We're No. 1!"

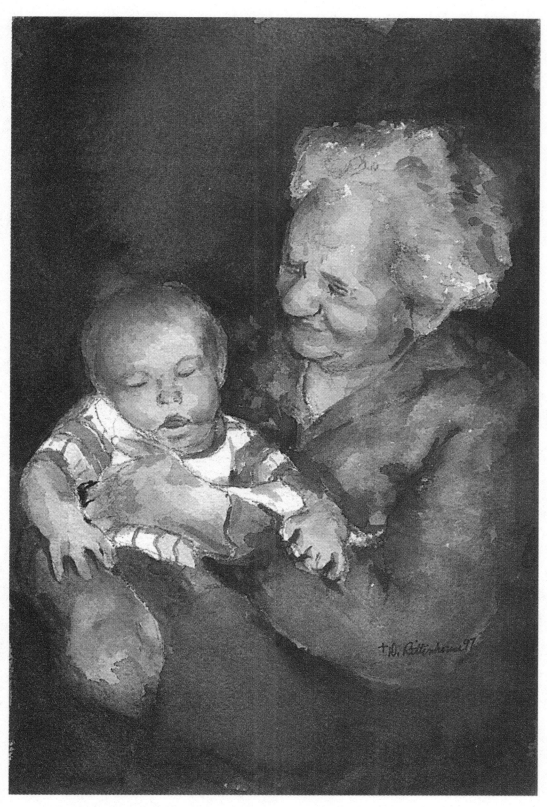

"Suffer the little children to come unto me...
for of such is the kingdom of God." Mark 10:14

"Look! The moon's broke."

Gabrielle was singing "Angels in the cereal!"
("Gloria in Excelsis Deo!").

Chapter Fourteen

Kids and Health

It often seems as though kids spend more time with runny noses, earaches, scraped knees, etc., than they do whole and healthy. Fortunately, kids seem to bounce back quickly from childhood illnesses and injuries — but you can't always say the same for the exhausted parents. The good news is that laughter is a great medicine. A sense of humor makes every challenge easier!

Like many children, Kelly had a tendency to get ear infections. The problem was especially bad when she went swimming, but her mother had learned that if she put a little alcohol in Kelly's ears after swimming, it helped to prevent the problem. One day Kelly's mom ran out of rubbing alcohol, so in desperation she grabbed a bottle of Scotch.

Not much later Kelly and her mom were waiting in line at the mall when a man started a conversation with Kelly.

"You are a very cute little girl," he told her.

"Thank you," she said brightly.

"You look like you have a little Scotch in you," he continued.

"Yes," Kelly replied. "My mother puts it in my ears when I go swimming!"

As Jordan, 7, was waiting for surgery her parents discussed the anesthesia process. Jordan asked what anesthesia is, but before her mother could answer, Jordan said, "I know what anesthesia is. It's one of Cinderella's wicked stepsisters!"

Katelyn overheard her mother talk about taking her older brother to the hospital for his booster shots. Later Katelyn told her preschool teacher, "Jonathan went to get bullets. I want to get bullets, too!"

Nathan, 4, did not like the new brand of breaded chicken pieces his mother had bought. He refused to eat them, but his mom said he had to eat at least one.

The next morning Nathan was itching all over.

"Nathan, I think you have chicken pox," his mother said.

"Mom, I knew you shouldn't have made me eat that chicken!" Nathan exclaimed.

Ron, 8, and Nathan, 5, like to make "experiments" by mixing up small amounts of spices, food coloring, soda, etc. One day Nathan handed his grandmother his latest experiment. "If you or Grandpa faint," he said, "just take some of this. After you throw up, you'll feel better!"

When Kyle was sick to his stomach and throwing up, he said, "Grandma, I swallowed UP!"

Jayden, 8, had told his mother he wasn't feeling very well. Later Logan, 6, came in from playing outside and the family sat down to dinner.

While they were eating, the boys' father commented that Jayden must be sick because he looked "awful green."

"Don't worry, Dad, if I look green," Logan said. "It's not because I'm sick. It's probably because I've been rolling around in the grass."

Paul, 9, wasn't feeling well. He complained that he had "growing pains."

Told that he should be grateful for growing pains, because they mean his bones are stretching and he's getting taller, Paul rubbed his forehead and said, "But I don't want my HEAD to get bigger!"

"Grandma, there's something I must tell you," Ron, 6, said. "I just got through wiping my runny nose on your pillow. But you don't need to worry. It will be all right. I turned it over!"

Alex, 5, broke a baby tooth. It was very jagged, so his mother took him to the dentist to have it removed.

The dentist said, "Alex, we'll just have to put that tooth to sleep, and when it's asleep we'll pull it, and you won't even know it."

Pretty soon the dentist walked to the reception area and told Alex's mother: "I put the Novocain into Alex's gum, and I waited a few minutes. Then I asked Alex, 'Is that tooth asleep yet?' And he said, 'No, but it's saying its prayers!'"

The doctor suggested that Shawn's parents put Vaseline on his nose at night to help keep his nostrils moist and prevent nosebleeds.

One night at bedtime, after the problem had stopped, Shawn told his parents that they had forgotten to "do the thing with gasoline."

They were puzzled.

"You know," Shawn said, "putting the gasoline in my nose so it won't bleed!"

Chapter Fourteen

When Brittney, 3, woke up in pain after having her tonsils removed, she looked at her mom and asked, "How could you let them do that to me?"

A family was on a long car trip with the 11-year-old and 8-year-old in the back seat. The mother nearly got whiplash from turning around when she heard her son say, "Keep doing that. You're a really good proctologist!" His sister was rubbing his feet.

At a large family Super Bowl party, Mary, 10, announced to all the people present: "I know why those football players are so big and so strong and have so many muscles — they take hemorrhoids!" (Her word for steroids!)

When a father broke his two front teeth, his little daughter asked eagerly whether she could take the two large chips to show and tell!

One morning at day care the children were comparing "boo-boos" that they had gotten over the weekend. Courtney showed where her cat had scratched her. Then she pointed to some cuts on her hand. With a great deal of thought and in all seriousness, she said, "I've had them since I was born!"

Amanda said she hated the medicine she had to take for her runny nose because it tasted like "dead cherries!"

Nancy phoned her husband, Gary, at work. When she gave the phone to Matt, 3, so he could talk to Daddy, he accidentally dropped the receiver on the hard tile floor.

"Dad, are you all right?" Matt asked anxiously as he picked the receiver up.

Austin told his dad about a very sad event at day care. A girl had to be picked up by ambulance and taken to the hospital.

When his father asked what the little girl's name was, Austin said, "I don't know. But the ambulance was a Ford!"

Jeremy, Ryan's friend, had to go to the doctor to get a TB booster shot. Jeremy excitedly told his family that Ryan had to get "a TV shot because he watches too much TV."

Liz announced to her parents that she had changed her career plans. She had decided to become a psychiatrist, because "they make lots of money and EVERYONE needs one!"

Chuck, 8, had been told to put on sunscreen, but when he came inside his face was beet red. His mother chided him for not following her instructions.

"I don't think it's a sunburn," Chuck said defensively. "It's just a real bad tan!"

A 4-year-old woke up feeling sick. She told her mother, "My throat is so sore it feels like I swallowed a bruise!"

Ben, 6, asked, "Mom, if someone is allergic to milk, does that mean they are allergic to cows, too?"

Kyle, 4, received careful emotional preparation for his upcoming ear surgery. In the recovery room where most of the children were crying because they were scared, Kyle was snoring softly. When he awakened, his first words were a pleasant "Is it all over?" As they wheeled him out in a wheelchair, which delighted him, he waved to the nurse, saying, "'Bye, I had a good time!"

His enthusiasm continued, and as his wheelchair ride continued he sang to the tune of "My Bonnie Lies Over the Ocean":

"Last night as I lay on my pillow, last night as I lay on my bed — I stuck my feet out the window. And now all my neighbors are dead!"

Azriela was feeling sick from something she had eaten. Noticing that her mother was turning green, Sarah, 2, asked, "Mommy, you sick?"

"Yes, Sarah, I have a tummy ache."

"Do you need a blanky?" Sarah asked.

"Sure, Sarah, that would make me feel better."

After giving her blanket to Azriela, Sarah asked, "You going to suck your thumb? Make you feel better."

Azriela pretended to suck her thumb. At that moment Sarah climbed onto her lap and said, "Here, Mom, have my thumb!" And she stuck her thumb into Azriela's mouth!

After a few sucks, Sarah declared: "You all better now!"

Azriela, who writes about relationships, says she learned two things from the thumb incident: 1. Don't overlook sources of support that you might not naturally think of. 2. People may try to comfort you by doing for you what works for them. What comforts you may be totally different than what comforts your spouse or children.

Chapter Fifteen

How Does Your Garden Grow?

There is nothing more gratifying than seeing a garden flourish after months of toil. Children are like the seeds that a gardener carefully plants. The soil is the nurturing that a family gives; the essential rain is the support that comes from a caring church and educational community; and the sunshine is God's love. As they grow and blossom, children brighten our lives with their wide-eyed but down-to-earth interpretation of Mother Nature's miracles.

Lisa, 4, lived near an elderly gentleman who spent many hours keeping his lawn beautifully manicured. After asking the man how he kept his yard so nice, Lisa came home with a great revelation. "Mom," she announced, "do you know how Mr. Lee keeps his yard so nice? He puts elbow grease on it!"

On a spring walk David, 5, noticed some bright yellow tulips with splashes of red on the inside.
"Look!" David exclaimed, "somebody painted the inside of those tulips!"

Shortly after Michael learned how to read, he found eggplant in a garden catalog.
"Hey, Mom," he said, "if you plant some of these we won't have to buy eggs any more!"

Seeing a sunflower for the first time, a 7-year-old boy said, "Mom, look at that huge dandelion!"

Chapter Fifteen

After playing with toy tractors for hours on his aunt's hardwood floors, Michael, 6, said, "Farming is hard on your knees!"

Peter, 3, was carefully studying the huge pine tree in his grandpa's back yard. It was laden with long, slim brown cones.

With great seriousness Peter asked, "Papa, how did those dog turds get up on that tree?"

Paul, 7, was helping his father work in the garden when he accidentally got some Miracle Gro on his finger. He showed his finger to his father and asked, "Is my finger going to get bigger?"

When Carolyn was a little girl she dearly loved strawberries. She saw them ripening in the backyard, and one day she started to pick them. "Carolyn, you can't eat those yet," her mother, Phyllis, said. "They're not sweet enough." Carolyn left the strawberry patch. Later Phyllis found Carolyn in the garden with a spoon, sprinkling sugar on the strawberry plants!

Little Phyllis was given some baby ducklings. They died and were buried in the garden, and Phyllis was very sad.

A few weeks later they found Phyllis watering the grave with a sprinkling can. She thought that if she watered them the ducks would come up!

Chuck, 2, was visiting his great-grandmother in a nursing home. They happened to leave when there was a long line of wheelchairs going down the hall, as the residents went to dinner. "I want to ride one of them tractors!" the farmer's son exclaimed.

Chapter Sixteen

Kids and Animals

Animals fascinate children. Whether they watch them on TV, see them at the zoo, play with them in the back yard or keep them indoors as pets, children embrace God's creatures — from whales to worms. One summer night a child came in with a handful of wriggling worms. When her mother told her to get rid of them Jessica exclaimed, "But Mom, they're my BEST FRIENDS!"

And probably at that moment they were!

Mike was taking Kelly Rose, 2, for a walk on a hot summer afternoon. It had rained hard the night before, leaving several earthworms stranded on the sidewalk.

Kelly stopped, bent down and began intensely studying one very dead worm that was dried to a crisp. Then she stood up and pronounced: "He needs to get some exercise!"

Kathy's dog was sick, and little Kyle asked her what she was going to do about it.

Trying to stick to language Kyle would understand, Kathy said she was going to take the dog to a "dog doctor."

Kyle's eyes opened wide, and he said, "I didn't know dogs could become doctors!"

Paul, 6, said he wanted to be a bowling instructor for Halloween.

"A bowling instructor?" Brenda asked in amazement.

"You know, Mom," Paul said. "That big snake!" (boa constrictor)

Chapter Sixteen

Brenda spotted her son Joel, 4, in the back yard playing with a big German shepherd.

"Joel," Brenda called in alarm, "don't play with that dog! You don't know him!"

"That's okay, Mom," Joel called back. "He doesn't know me either."

Bobby, 3, was fishing with Brenda. She scooped up some of the water by the shoreline for the bucket with the fish that had been caught. It was a windy day, and the water was quite muddy.

"Grandma," Bobby exclaimed, "how come you put the fish in chocolate water?"

Brittni said, "Now Grandma, don't laugh. But I think a mosquito bit me on the tongue last night!"

Taylor was teasing one of the cats. The cat was getting angry, and his tail was flicking back and forth. Taylor's mom told him to leave the cat alone. When the teasing stopped, the cat stopped flicking its tail.

"Look, Mom," Taylor said, "his batteries are dead!"

A family was snowmobiling in Michigan on the Blue Bear Trail. After they had been out quite a while, Sue told Brody, 7, it was time to go back. Brody protested that it was too soon. "I haven't seen a blue bear yet!" he said.

Gretchen told Aaron, 5, that the goldfish in his aquarium were probably raised on a goldfish farm. "You mean someone didn't catch them with a fishing pole and take them to Wal-Mart?" he asked.

When she saw her grandpa cleaning fish for the first time, Brenda, 3, said, "I get the gizzard!"

While Dana, 7, was reading a book about a ladybug, she paused and asked her mother: "Why are there no man bugs?"

Cindy showed her preschool students a picture of a sheep. "Does anyone know what this is?" she asked.
"It's a baaaaaaat!" said 4-year-old Zachary.

Alexander told his grandparents that his new dog was a bugle.
His grandparents explained to him that the word is beagle.
The next time he told about his dog, he said proudly, "She's an EAGLE!"

Chelsey said, "Did you know that when dogs kiss, they drain?" She meant drool!

Chuck, 6, said he was going to name the toad he found Toady Come Home. "That way he'll know what to do when I call him!" Chuck explained.

Kim was telling her grandpa about her Yorkie, which has a very long tongue. "I think when they cut his tail, they really pushed it in, and it came out a long tongue instead," she said.

Chapter Sixteen

A pastor's wife invited Phyllis, Sara and Nancy to see their hamster family. As the pastor's wife showed off the new hamster babies, she told about their habits.

Sara, 6, was strangely quiet. But when she got to the car she exploded. "Our preacher. I hate him. I hate him," she said.

"Sara, what a terrible thing to say," her mother reprimanded.

"Oh, Mother," Sara said, lifting her suffering eyes. "Didn't you hear the pastor's wife say that when there are new babies she must be very fast to get them away or the father will eat them all? I hate him!"

Jonathan, 5, memorized the names of 50 birds. One day while they were driving he pointed to a martin house and told his mother, "There is one thing I can't understand. How do those birds build those houses, Mom?"

While Doris was leading a preschool story time, the children enjoyed observing a rabbit in a large cardboard box. One of the little boys looked into the box and told Doris, "You didn't tell me rabbits eat blueberries!"

"They don't eat blueberries."

"But there are blueberries in the box," the little boy protested.

Guess what Rebecca named the bluebird she got for Christmas? Pinky.

Paul, 10, was reading "Mr. Popper's Penguins" out loud to me. All of a sudden he stopped. "Mom, I've got a question," he said. "Do they kill penguins for their tuxedos?"

Chapter Seventeen

Turning Boys into Men

"Success is peace of mind in knowing that you did your best." John Wooden, basketball coach, UCLA.

During the days before the youth baseball league tournament I kept telling myself that the outcome didn't matter. For our team, the important things had already happened. Our 8- and 9-year-olds had become much better hitters — in practice, at least. They were better at catching the ball, and they were developing good instincts about what to do with it when they had it. They had proved their dedication by showing up for extra practices. They were having fun. And they had a winning record that any team would be proud of.

"You're getting better," their coach — my husband — told them time and time again. "But you're not the best. You are practicing and trying to get better. Practice is what will make the difference." He was proud of their work so far. But he was urging them to go the extra mile. He wanted them to prove that they could be champions.

That's a lot of pressure to put on grade-school boys and girls. They might be pretty good athletes. But playing in a tournament creates stress. Learning to deal with it is part of growing up, I guess. But I'm 44 years young, and I was stressed out too!

"I don't care who wins or loses," I prayed. "Just let the kids play their best. Let them be proud of how they play."

As we went into the championship round of the double-elimination tournament, our opponent had one tournament loss and we didn't have any. Therefore, if we lost the first game we would have a second chance for victory. The bad news was that our opponent had some tremendous hitters and was averaging about a dozen runs a game. So the key would be defense.

In the first inning our opponents had a three-run homer. We rallied, but lost the game, 8-7.

Chapter Seventeen

In the dugout, our team looked dazed and demoralized. Several kids were crying. A few of the parents tried to console them. "Come on, you guys, get your chins up!" one mom said. "You can do it! That first game was just practice!" another mom said. But the entire team looked glum.

Then we won the coin toss to decide which team was the home team for the second game. Terry came over to the dugout beaming. "They called heads, and it was tails!" he told the crestfallen crew. "Tails! That means we're going to whip their tails!" There was laughter. Humor worked where other kinds of encouragement had failed. The re-energized team raced onto the field, ready to play.

In the first inning we held the opponents to one run. When it was our turn at bat, Lauren, our left-handed first baseman, hit a two-run homer, his third of the year. After the cheering died down, Lauren's mom, who was sitting behind me, said, with mock dismay, "Oh, darn! Now I owe him $10...Well, maybe he'll forget!"

Lauren's two-run homer gave us the lead. More important, it gave us the confidence we needed to play our best. We didn't score in the next two innings, but neither did the other team. They were hitting, but we stopped their hits.

We went into the bottom of the fourth still leading, 2-1. And then something amazing happened. One by one, with assembly-line precision, each of our 11 players marched to home plate and had a hit or drove in runs. You could feel their confidence growing. The hours and hours of extra batting practice were paying off. One by one the kids were showing their stuff. We won, 10-2!

Many of our players — and their parents — will remember that win for a lifetime. Few, if any, of the kids will become great baseball players, so the victory had nothing to do with heralding the start of great baseball careers. But it had everything to do with proving to the kids the value of practice, teamwork, and not giving up. There's no magic formula. Practice, teamwork and confidence won't always lead to wins. But, as their coaches told them for three months, you can't be a winner without them.

Chapter Eighteen

Kids and Sports

Sports are for the young and the young at heart. If you aren't physically able to play ball, bowl, swim, golf, sled or skate with a child, spend some time watching him or her at play. You may get a workout just from laughing!

A little boy was playing pee-wee baseball for the first time. The tiniest boy on the team, he came to every practice and to every game, but try as he might, he could never hit the ball. One day a miracle happened. The pitcher aimed straight for the little boy's bat, and the ball hit the bat.

With great joy and amazement, the boy ran to first base. When he got there he looked up at the coach who was standing by the base and asked, "What do I do now? I've never been here before!"

Eight-year-old cousins Alex and Andrew were playing golf with putters and a plastic golf ball.

Alex, who was fairly adept at the game, hit the ball and yelled, "Fore!"

Andrew took his turn. He hit the ball and yelled, "FORD!"

When Greg was coaching soccer for kindergarteners, one of the players, Sarah, came up to him halfway through a game and said, "Teacher, teacher! We need to stop. I'm starting to sweat!"

Chapter Eighteen

At his first East Noble High School basketball game, Ian, 4, was confused by one of the cheers.

As the home crowd roared, "Let's go, E-N!" Ian turned to his parents and asked, "Why are they yelling my name?"

Anthony, 5, was with his Uncle Terry in the toy department. Anthony saw Terry looking at a boomerang and asked him what it does.

"When you throw it, the boomerang will come back to you," Terry said.

Anthony looked concerned. "Isn't that kinda dangerous?" he asked.

Adam, 5, flipped on the television just as one of the NBA games between the Utah Jazz and the Chicago Bulls was ending. His dad called from the other room, asking what the score was.

"Ninety-seven to 85," Adam replied.

"Who won?" his dad asked.

"Ninety-seven," Adam replied.

Paul, 8, was on a team that had lost twice to a team called Musselman's.

I told Paul that if he really tried hard his team could beat Musselman's.

"No, we can't," he said.

"Yes, you can," I said. "If you really try."

"Mom, don't you know," he said. "They're the MUSCLE MEN!"

Funny Kids

A little boy at the Topeka ball diamond was overheard saying: "I whacked it. And I hit it! It was a miracle!"

When Nathan played T-ball for the first time, his grandma asked him whether he got a hit. "Yes," Nathan replied. Then he added defensively, "But he hit me first!"

Once, Nathan said he got to fourth base!

When Isabella, 3, missed the ball her father kicked to her she exclaimed, "The ball didn't know where I was!"

Tiffany, 5, was not enjoying the high school football game. At halftime, she asked if they could go home.

Her dad said, "Just one more quarter, and then we'll leave."

Tiffany pulled a quarter from her pocket and said, "Here's one. Can we go now?"

Paul, 7, told Terry he was thinking about selling some of his baseball cards.

"Don't sell them," Terry said. "Some day they will be worth a lot of money. Keep them, and then if you need to you can sell them to get money for college."

Paul thought a minute. "I don't think I'll sell them," he said. "I think I'll keep them so that when I am old and in a nursing home I can have my baseball cards beside my bed!"

Peter, 8, told about an exciting basketball game where the fans threw graffiti. (He meant confetti.)

The junior varsity basketball team won, but the varsity team lost. As they were leaving the high school Jeff, 5, said happily, "That was a really fair game. They won one, and we won one!"

Shawn told his dad the Sunday afternoon football game was the Lions playing the Big Green Peppers (Green Bay Packers)!

Dustin, 7, was getting ready to swim in Lake Wawasee, the largest natural lake in Indiana. Before he jumped in, he asked cautiously, "Is there any chlorine in here?"

A second-grader said, "Last summer I drowned a little bit. Then I drowned all the way. Then my uncle saved me!"

While watching the swimmers in the Summer Olympics, Joeb, 3, said, "Mommy, I want to swim. We need to go buy me some little underwear!" (a Speedo)

Jarod said he couldn't hit the ball because his eyes were asleep.

Paul, 7, went to a basketball camp. Asked whether he was looking forward to playing basketball in high school, he said no. He said he wanted to go straight to the NBA!

Chapter Nineteen

The Most Important Goal

A soggy Sunday afternoon soccer game gave new meaning to the sermon I had heard that morning in church.

It started spitting rain half an hour before our son's second soccer game of the day. By the time play started, water was coming down in sheets. Wet and chilled to the bone, my husband and I headed for the car, hoping that maybe we could watch from inside our vehicle. But all we could see was just a gray blur.

After about five minutes we moved the car to a position behind one of the goals, where the viewing was much easier. The windshield wipers were swishing furiously. I had to wipe the inside of the windshield every few minutes, because the defrosting system wasn't working. The wipers, the fog on the windshield, and the driving rain made everything hazy. But I could tell that the 10-year-olds were not letting the weather dampen their enthusiasm. They were giving it all they had. I saw my son constantly working himself into the middle of the action. They had lost the first game, and I knew how desperately he and his teammates wanted to win.

As the game wore on it appeared there was going to be a 0-0 tie, which to our players would seem the same as losing. Our players were in control of the ball and attempting many shots, but none were successful.

I felt sorry for our team. They were struggling as hard as they could, but the weather and the other team's skillful play made it seem like a goal was impossible.

I was discouraged about losing two games in one day. Wouldn't it be wonderful, I thought, if the score really were 1-0 and we were ahead, but I didn't know it? That only happens in books and movies, I chided myself.

Then, all of a sudden, the players were running off the field. My son came to the car and told us that the game was going to be called off because lightning had been seen.

"We won!" he added.

"You did?" I said in amazement. "I thought it was 0-0."

"We got two goals at the beginning," he said. "Didn't you see them?"

I realized that at the beginning of the game our car had been too far away for us to see a goal being made.

That evening, as I mulled over the day's two main events — church and then soccer — it dawned on me that the soggy soccer game illustrated a biblical principle. Day by day we watch and struggle, often in damp and dismal situations, as we and others try to "win" the game of life. We try our hardest. Sometimes we get tired and feel sorry for ourselves and others.

But the discouragement goes away and we receive new strength when we realize the battle is already won. Our 10-year-old soccer players didn't give up. They knew they were winning, but they never stopped trying. I, peering through the fog and rain, was the one who gave up, because I hadn't seen the beginning of the game. We didn't see Christ's victory — His winning goal for all mankind — but through Christ we are victors. And through the Holy Spirit we know of that victory and have the faith and strength we need to spread the good news!

Chapter Twenty

Kids and Christmas

The best Christmases are those that are spent with children. Their excitement and wonder give new brightness and meaning to the traditional services and festivities!

At a Christmas Eve program, Ann's 5-year-old grandson bent over and whispered, "Grandma, why doesn't that baby Jesus ever get any older? I've been to five of these programs!"

Nathan was excited to be an angel in the Christmas pageant at church. He quickly got into his white, flowing costume, jumped up on a chair, waved his arms wildly — and then plummeted to the floor on his face.

Somewhat abashed, he picked himself up and asked, "Grandma, do you think you could find a chair that is a little bit higher, so that I can get my bearings and make a better landing?"

Jade, 2, was repeatedly told not to touch the fancy ornaments on the Christmas tree. When Gary caught her playing with the delicate decorations, he yelled at her.

"I didn't mean to," Jade said, bursting into tears. "I'm sorry. I'm just learning!"

Rebecca, 5, said she thought the Christmas tree must be a girl because it has a skirt.

Adam, 4, sang "Frosty the Snowman" this way: "...with a torn tob pipe and a runny nose..."

When Bee took the children to see Santa, little Luke said, "Bee, that wasn't the real Santa. It was just one of the elves, because he said 'Hey, Dude,' and the real Santa wouldn't say 'Hey, Dude!'"

Told that her church was going to have a float in the Christmas parade, Carrie, 4, asked, "Where will the water be?"

Cathie took Scott, 4, Christmas shopping. They bought the video "Willy Wonka and the Chocolate Factory" for a family Christmas present. Later they wrapped it and put it under the tree, and Cathie stressed to Scott the importance of not telling anyone what it was.

When Fred came home that night Scott showed his dad the wrapped present. Fred said he was going to try to guess what it was.

Scott immediately told him, "It's NOT 'Willy Wonka and the Chocolate Factory!'"

Bobby, 7, told Santa that all he wanted for Christmas was an elf.

"Why do you want an elf?" Santa asked with surprise.

"Because I have lots of broken toys," Bobby said. "And my brother needs an elf, too, because he has more broken toys than I do!"

Rachel, 5, was in charge of putting the Christmas seals on the back of the Christmas-card envelopes. When one seal would not stick, Rachel said, "Mom, I think I put too much lick on this one!"

The night of the Christmas program, little Ron wanted to back out. But when he saw the beautiful angel wings he would be wearing he decided to stick it out. He laughed and said shakily, "First I had butterflies in my stomach, and now I am becoming one!"

Tiffany, 7, was helping her grandmother put the lights on the Christmas tree.

"I don't think I like the way the tree looks," Nancy said, stepping back to check her work.

"Don't worry, Grandma," Tiffany said. "It will look better after we put on the garlic (garland)."

Carrie, 3, was asked what her baby sister Mollie wanted for Christmas.

"She's not getting anything," Carrie said. "She's just a baby, and she can't tell Santa what she wants."

Elizabeth, 6, was writing a Christmas list. She wanted to ask for a video. "How do you spell VCR?" she asked.

Megan told her library teacher, "Santa says 'Ho, ho, ho!' Mama says, 'No, no, no!'"

"Why do they say Merry Christmas?" Katie's granddad asked her. "They say Happy Thanksgiving, Happy Easter and Happy Birthday. Merry doesn't go with Christmas."

The 6-year-old looked at her grandfather seriously. "But, Papa," she said. "Mary does go with Christmas. She was the mother of Jesus!"

Jake, 5, heard the song "I Saw Mommy Kissing Santa Claus" and started singing along with it. Then he climbed on his grandma's lap and said, "I sure hope my dad don't catch Santa kissing my mom. If he did he would beat him up, and I wouldn't get any presents at all!"

Rachel, 3, was elated when she was told she could be a "star" in the Christmas program. But then she was worried. "Mom," she asked, "how will they get me way up in the sky?"

A few weeks before Christmas a 3-year-old was watching his mother undress.

"Can Santa see me now?" he asked his mother.

"Yes," she said.

"Can he see you now?" he asked.

"Yes," she said.

"Well, I know what he'd say if he could see you now," the 3-year-old said. "Wooooooo-EEEEEEE! Look at them buns!"

Lindsay, 6, told her mom: "I believe in Santa Claus. And I believe in the elves. But those flying deer. I don't buy those flying deer!"

Chapter Twenty-One

Learning the Truth About Santa

Learning the truth about Santa is one of life's turning points. Some kids, like my oldest, try to postpone that event as long as possible. Now, 13 years after she said, "Santa Claus is a fake," I think she would still classify herself as a believer.

"Santa Claus is a fake."

I felt numb as my tousle-haired 5-year-old looked up from the bug book she was leafing through and made her pronouncement.

"Who told you that?" I asked in my calmest manner.

"No one. I just know he is."

"Why do you think so?"

"I don't think he brings all the presents."

"Oh."

End of conversation. Dolly resumed perusing her book about bugs, and I sat on the sofa, thinking.

About a quarter of a century ago, I, too, had my initial doubts. I remember as a 5- or 6-year-old helping my mother dry dishes and pestering her with questions, "How does Santa visit all the children in one night? How does he get into the homes without chimneys? Why doesn't he bring me everything I ask for...or at least give me as much as he gives Cindy (my friend down the street)?"

Finally, my mother gave in and admitted there isn't really a Santa Claus. He's a symbol of the love and caring that Christmas is all about.

I wasn't crestfallen. I was glad she had told me the truth. I had had doubts, had come to her with my questions, and she had given me the facts. I could continue to count on Mom.

But that Christmas had a little less sparkle than the previous ones. I felt older and wiser...knowing that when we looked out the window on Christmas Eve there wasn't a chance of seeing a sleigh and eight flying reindeer...knowing that the cookies and milk I put out with my younger sisters and brother would be enjoyed by my parents...knowing there was no hope of receiving more expensive gifts than my parents could afford.

I have always said when our children ask whether there is a Santa Claus I won't lie. If you lie and they find out the truth later from their friends, they won't trust you on more important things.

But Dolly's comment that "Santa Claus is a fake" didn't seem like a question. It didn't seem like she needed...or wanted...an answer.

Maybe in the coming weeks she'll pose the question directly. Even though she points to the North Pole on the globe and tells her 3-year-old sister that's where Santa lives, I think deep down inside she is beginning to doubt the jolly man's existence.

So if she asks again why I pick up used toys at the Toys for Tots 'n Teens collection boxes and help clean them up, instead of saying Welcome Wagon is helping Santa, I'll probably say Welcome Wagon is BEING Santa for parents who are having hard times.

I'll probably add that although Santa isn't real, he represents the good and caring people who give of themselves. I'll say he represents the Christmas spirit that lives in people's hearts.

This year or next year I wonder how she'll react. Will she take the news calmly and with a certain sense of relief, as I did? Will she, like my husband, not even remember the revelation? Or will she react like my brother-in-law?

Upon learning from his mother there isn't a Santa, he immediately fired back, "What about the Easter Bunny?"

My mother-in-law nodded.

"Oh, no, not him, too!" Gary wailed. It was almost too much to bear.

So Wilma decided to wait a while before breaking him the news about the Tooth Fairy.

Chapter Twenty-Two

Bedtime Blues

"Now I lay me down to sleep..." If only it were that easy! Every parent has had at least a few struggles getting the little ones to quiet down. Late one night Gary was rocking his granddaughter, Jade, 2, in the living room. He could hardly keep his eyes open. He had done everything he could think of to get her to go to sleep.

"Are you sleepy?" Jade, who was wide awake, asked Gary.

"Yes, I am," Gary answered.

"Then why don't you go to your own bed?" Jade asked.

Yes, the Sandman comes, but often he reaches the parents and grandparents first!

Early one morning after her father had left for work, Ariel, 3, asked Sabrina whether she could get into bed with her. Sabrina said it would be fine.

As she lay beside her mother, Ariel kept talking. Sabrina told her it was time to be quiet and to get back to sleep.

Ariel lay still. The room was quiet except for the loud ticking of the clock.

"But, Mom," Ariel said after a few minutes, "your clock won't go to sleep!"

Jeanna, 5, had trouble falling to sleep. Her mother, Rosemary, told her to say a little prayer to God and then "pretend you are on a farm and counting sheep."

A little while later Jeanna reported she still couldn't fall asleep.

"Didn't you count sheep?" Rosemary asked.

"Yes, but they ran out!"

When she was a little girl, Joyce wondered who that awful man, Harmon Danger, was. When her mother said bedtime prayers with the children, she always closed with: "And dear Lord, please keep us all safe from harm and danger!"

Logan, 5, told his mother that when he goes to bed at night he lies awake all night and never sleeps.
Jayden, 7, asked, "Well, what do you do all night then?"
Logan replied, "I just lie there and watch my dreams!"

Chuck, 8, told his mother very seriously one morning, "I started to have a bad dream last night. But I woke myself up and I changed the channels!"

Susan woke little Zane up from his nap, and he was angry. "You popped my dream," he said.

Karen was going to move a little girl who had fallen asleep in front of the TV. When the little girl woke up, she said she didn't want to go to her bedroom.
"But you were asleep," Karen said.
"No," the little girl said, "I was just resting my eyes!"

Kyle took a nap with his grandma. In the middle of their nap, he woke her up. "You were HONKING!" he explained.
Grandma was puzzled. Then she realized she had been snoring.

When she was tucking Evan, 2, into bed, Kim told him, "I love you to pieces."

"I love you together," Evan said.

Looking at the moon with his mother, Jonathan said, "Mom, look, the moon is caught on a cloud...How are they going to get it unstuck?"

Anna, 4, was working at the dining-room table. When she got up after finishing her project she exclaimed, "My foot just fell asleep without me!"

When his father, George, was active in politics, David, 4, often went on overnight trips with him.

Once he overheard George telling David's mother, Dianne, to pack pajamas for David "because we'll be sleeping on the road."

David was worried. "Dad," he said, "I don't think I want to sleep ON the road!"

Little Victoria was exhausted after a day at the county fair. "My feet are tired. My legs are tired. Even my hair is tired," she said.

When Scott, 4, saw the rising sun streaming through his brother's bedroom window he said, "Mom, Dustin's window has the morning on it!"

Chapter Twenty-Two

One day Paul lost two teeth. He put both of them, plus a shark's tooth, under his pillow.

When Terry came to tuck him in, he noticed a strong scent, and asked Paul why he had put on aftershave lotion.

"For the Tooth Fairy," Paul said.

When Grandma DeCamp said goodbye to Elizabeth, 2, she said it was late and time for the Sandman to come.

"He's going to put new sand in my sandbox!" Elizabeth said with excitement.

Kathy woke up Andrew for school one January day. Although it was 7 a.m. it was still pitch black outside.

Rubbing his eyes, Andrew said, "It's so dark. Are they going to cancel school?"

Kenny called to Billy, 2, and said, "Look at that beautiful crescent moon."

Billy looked for a moment and then said softly, "The moon's broke!"

Chapter Twenty-Three

A Tear and a Smile

"The heavens cry when angels depart." (Yugoslavian proverb)

I never imagined we would take our firstborn to college during cold, steady, relentless rain. I assumed the August day would be sunny, hot and sticky, the way it was every moving day when I was a student at Indiana University, two decades ago.

As we dodged puddles while loading the minivan, I told my daughter that the rain reminded me of a proverb an old Yugoslav had told me when I left his home in a downpour back in the days when I was a student traveler. But she wasn't even curious to know what the proverb was. Her mind was on other things — such as how to get all her gear into our vehicle and packed around three squirming siblings whom she didn't want to take along.

But the driving rain was only a small surprise when compared to what we discovered when we arrived at Hillsdale College. An electrical malfunction just 24 hours before our arrival had caused a fire that made our daughter's dormitory temporarily uninhabitable. The fire had caused so much smoke damage that Olds Residence, where 84 freshman girls were to be housed, wouldn't be ready for use for two to three weeks.

So instead of moving our daughter into a dorm, we moved her into a room at the Days Inn — a double room that she would share with three other refugees. (Two girls to a bed.) They would be shuttled back and forth to the campus for classes, meals and other activities. Because the two-bed room had only two drawers, one desk and one tiny closet, the girls could keep only a few changes of clothes and some toilet articles. Everything else they had brought for their first "home away from home" had to be put in labeled garbage bags in a storage area that Hillsdale officials had arranged. Then, when Olds Residence was ready for residents, the garbage bags would be delivered.

At the opening convocation, college President Dr. George Roche told the parents (nearly half of the freshman girls were affected) that it's best to look at the fire and the displacement it caused as an opportunity. Maybe it will cause a special bonding among the girls, he suggested. Perhaps at future college reunions they'll call themselves the "Days Inn Group." (The "DAZED Inn Group" fluttered through my mind.)

One of the things I was most looking forward to was keeping in touch with our daughter through e-mail. Like most colleges and universities these days, Hillsdale provides free e-mail accounts for its students. Some parents have told me they communicate more with their children via e-mail than they did when they were all together under the same roof.

I wanted to hear how the "Dazed Inn Group" is doing, what her classes are like, and how basketball is going. I wanted to know how her first load of wash comes out...

When I found myself starting to worry, I recalled one of the farewells we overheard. After a hug, a freshman girl thought of something she wanted her parents to get for her.

"Well," her father said in a kindly voice, "you can get it at Wal-Mart. That's what adults do — they solve their own problems!"

Our Family Stories

"This is the day which the Lord has made; we will rejoice and be glad in it."

(Psalms 118:24)

Our Family Stories

Our Family Stories

Our Family Stories

Order Form

If you would like more copies of "The Funny Things Kids Say" for yourself or for a friend please use this form. If your book is from the library, please photocopy this form.

Name _____

Address _____

Phone number _____

Please send

    _____copies of Vol. 1 of "The Funny Things Kids Say"
    _____copies of Vol. 2 of "The Funny Things Kids Say"
    _____copies of Vol. 3 of "The Funny Things Kids Say"

Softcover copies are $15 each. That price includes **FREE Priority** Mail shipping. If you are an Indiana resident, please add sales tax.

    Amount enclosed: _____
    (Make check payable to: Funny Kids Project)

    Mail to:
    Funny Kids Project
    816 Mott St.
    Kendallville, IN 46755 USA

The books will be autographed! Please include any special autographing instructions. Matted, signed illustrations from the books are also available. Call 219-347-0738 for information.

Thank you for buying our books and pictures! Satisfaction guaranteed or your money back!